Alaska: The Land and the People

Alaska: The Land and the People

by

EVELYN I. BUTLER

and

GEORGE A. DALE

Illustrated with Photographs

THE VIKING PRESS • New York

PUBLISHED IN 1957 BY THE VIKING PRESS, INC.
625 MADISON AVENUE, NEW YORK 22, N. Y.

PUBLISHED IN CANADA BY THE MACMILLAN COMPANY OF CANADA LIMITED

SECOND PRINTING 1958

LITHOGRAPHED IN U.S.A.

Contents

Foreword		7
Chapter I	Alaska in the Neighborhood of Nations	13
II	The Country	19
III	The People	29
IV	Life in a Small Coastal Village	42
V	With the Eskimos	63
VI	Arctic Reindeer Round-up	97
VII	Life in an Interior Indian Village	108
VIII	The Larger Towns	142

Acknowledgments

Most of the photographs in this book were taken by George A. Dale. For those taken by other photographers, and reproduced here by permission, the authors extend thanks to: the Bureau of Indian Affairs and William Darden, photographer, for the pictures on pages 33, 69, 71, and 92; Clara H. Gaddie, Seattle, Washington, for the picture on page 28; the Geophysical Institute, the University of Alaska, for the picture on page 140; J. Malcolm Greany, Juneau, Alaska, for the pictures on pages 20, 21, 22, 120, and 146; the Ketchikan Chamber of Commerce and Otto C. Schallerer, photographer, for the pictures on pages 43 and 148; Griffin's Photo, Fairbanks, Alaska, for the pictures on pages 36 and 145; Northwest Airlines and Ward W. Wells, photographer, for the picture on page 143; The Photo Shop Studio, Sitka, Alaska, for the picture on page 150; the United States Department of the Interior and Ray B. Dame, photographer, for the pictures on pages 45 and 53; the United States Fish and Wildlife Service, for the pictures on pages 73 and 120; Maxcine Williams, Juneau, Alaska, for the picture on page 44; and Wyman's Photo Service, Fairbanks, Alaska, for the pictures on pages 116 and 153.

Foreword

George Dale and Evelyn Butler (his wife) are two of the best-qualified people I know to discuss Alaska. For more than a dozen years both were connected with the education work of the Alaska Native Service (Bureau of Indian Affairs in Alaska).* First as Supervisors of Elementary Education, later with George as Director of Native Education and Evelyn as Director of Native Welfare, both were brought into frequent contact with realities in all parts of the territory. Neither was an armchair administrator; both were active field people. They toured the native villages in midwinter, while school was in session, with sleeping bag and field pack, traveling between stations by dog team when necessary. Later came the bush pilot and two-seater, hedge-hopping airplane, with George sitting next to the pilot, often guiding him on his first visit to some out-of-the-way clump of sod igloos, half covered with snow, and advising him where the white expanse was likely to be underlaid with something solid for skis to traverse and rest on.

George knew not only the teachers but the native children and their parents as well, and he was able to sit down with his native

* Unlike the people of most colonial territories, the Alaskan Eskimos, Aleuts, and Indians do not resent the term "native." In fact, the designation "Alaska Native Service" was adopted at the suggestion of the natives to define the several peoples helped by the Indian Service in Alaska.

hosts to a meal of smoked salmon, mucktuck, and salmon berries in seal oil with good appetite. Most white Alaskans find the native diet a little hard to take; and, as everywhere else in the world, inability to share common food rears a barrier that is difficult to surmount even with the best will in the world. I remember only one occasion when native food got the better of George. He and Evelyn were taking a short tour between Anchorage and Matanuska, as administrators of the Eklutna Boarding School. (This school is now closed.) It was during the summer, and, as most of the student body remained on campus, George had organized them into fishing crews to seine for salmon in the Knik Arm of Cook Inlet, on which the school fronts. As the salmon catch was brought ashore, the fish were beheaded, cleaned, and either smoked or salted by the girl students. At the end of the season a big fish feed was arranged, which started with salmon-head chowder. George sat down quite calmly, for most of the menu consisted of food with which he was familiar. However, when his bowl of chowder was set before him, and he looked down at it to find his stare returned by several calm, unblinking salmon eyes, George retired in defeat.

It was George's familiarity with the trail that made him quick to appreciate why an old Eskimo shop teacher, employed to teach boys how to make and repair snowshoes and sled runners, emphatically rejected an automatic push drill, offered him by the school's white principal. This was intended to replace the primitive Eskimo bow-drill, in which holes are bored in wood with a rusty nail twirled with a rawhide thong held in tension by a wooden bow. The old teacher explained that to break a snowshoe on the trail and be unable to repair it might cost a man or boy his life. Eskimos do not own and cannot afford automatic drills of the kind he had been proffered. Anyone who allowed himself to become dependent on such a gadget was a fool, the old teacher said, and would pay for his folly with his life. Any Eskimo has a nail, which fact the old man demonstrated by pulling an assortment from his own pocket. With his ever-present knife he could cut a bit of willow or other wood for a bow, and with a piece of snowshoe thong make himself an adequate drill to repair his snowshoe, or make a new one.

During George's stay in Alaska, the Alaska Native Service operated one hundred and eighteen schools, most of them in small native villages. George has been to all of them, not once but several times—from Barrow to Ketchikan, from Attu (in the Aleutians) to Eagle (on the Yukon near the Canadian border)—at all seasons of the year. What George writes about he illustrates with photographs which he himself has taken, because he was there in person.

There aren't many men today who possess such extensive first-hand experience with all phases of Alaska life; fewer still who are also artists with the camera; none who know and love Alaska and Native Alaskans more sincerely.

WILLARD W. BEATTY
Former Director of Education
Bureau of Indian Affairs
United States Department of Interior

Alaska: The Land and the People

CHAPTER I

Alaska in the Neighborhood of Nations

If you could ride a rocket ship straight up from the North Pole to a point many miles out in space, you could look back and see the earth as a great globe. It would appear many times larger than the biggest Halloween moon—bigger than any of the heavenly bodies that can be seen from the earth. The continents and land masses would look something like those shown on the maps on the next pages.

On the polar map it is easy to see why Alaska is a stop-over point on the new transpolar air flights between the two hemispheres, the eastern and the western; between Europe and the United States; and, of course, between Asia and the United States. Traveling by way of the recently established air routes over the North Pole, one may leave Copenhagen about nine o'clock Saturday evening, have early-Sunday-morning coffee at Anchorage, Alaska, and be in Tokyo for luncheon on Monday. Alaska has a distinctive role as Uncle Sam's hostess to international guests traveling on the new global express planes. The world's greatest airlines are featuring these trips by way of the well-advertised "Polar Short Cut—through the realm of the Midnight Sun and Aurora Borealis."

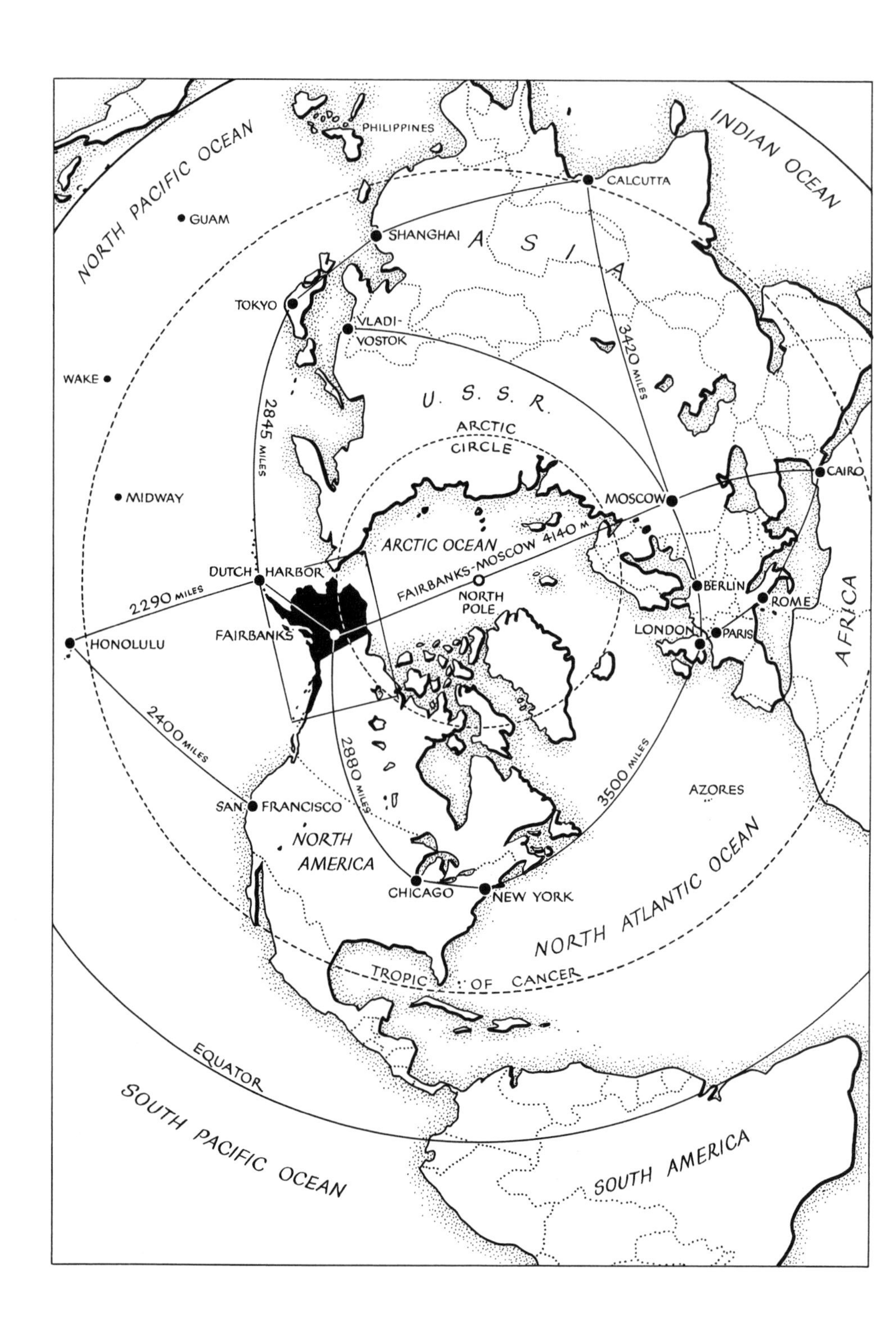

NORTH PACIFIC OCEAN
PHILIPPINES
INDIAN OCEAN
CALCUTTA
GUAM
SHANGHAI
A S I A
TOKYO
VLADI-
VOSTOK
3420 MILES
WAKE
U. S. S. R.
2845 MILES
ARCTIC
CIRCLE
MIDWAY
MOSCOW
CAIRO
ARCTIC OCEAN
FAIRBANKS-MOSCOW 4140 M
DUTCH HARBOR
NORTH
POLE
BERLIN
2290 MILES
ROME
FAIRBANKS
LONDON
PARIS
AFRICA
HONOLULU
2400 MILES
2880 MILES
3500 MILES
AZORES
SAN FRANCISCO
NORTH
AMERICA
NORTH ATLANTIC OCEAN
CHICAGO
NEW YORK
TROPIC OF CANCER
EQUATOR
SOUTH PACIFIC OCEAN
SOUTH AMERICA

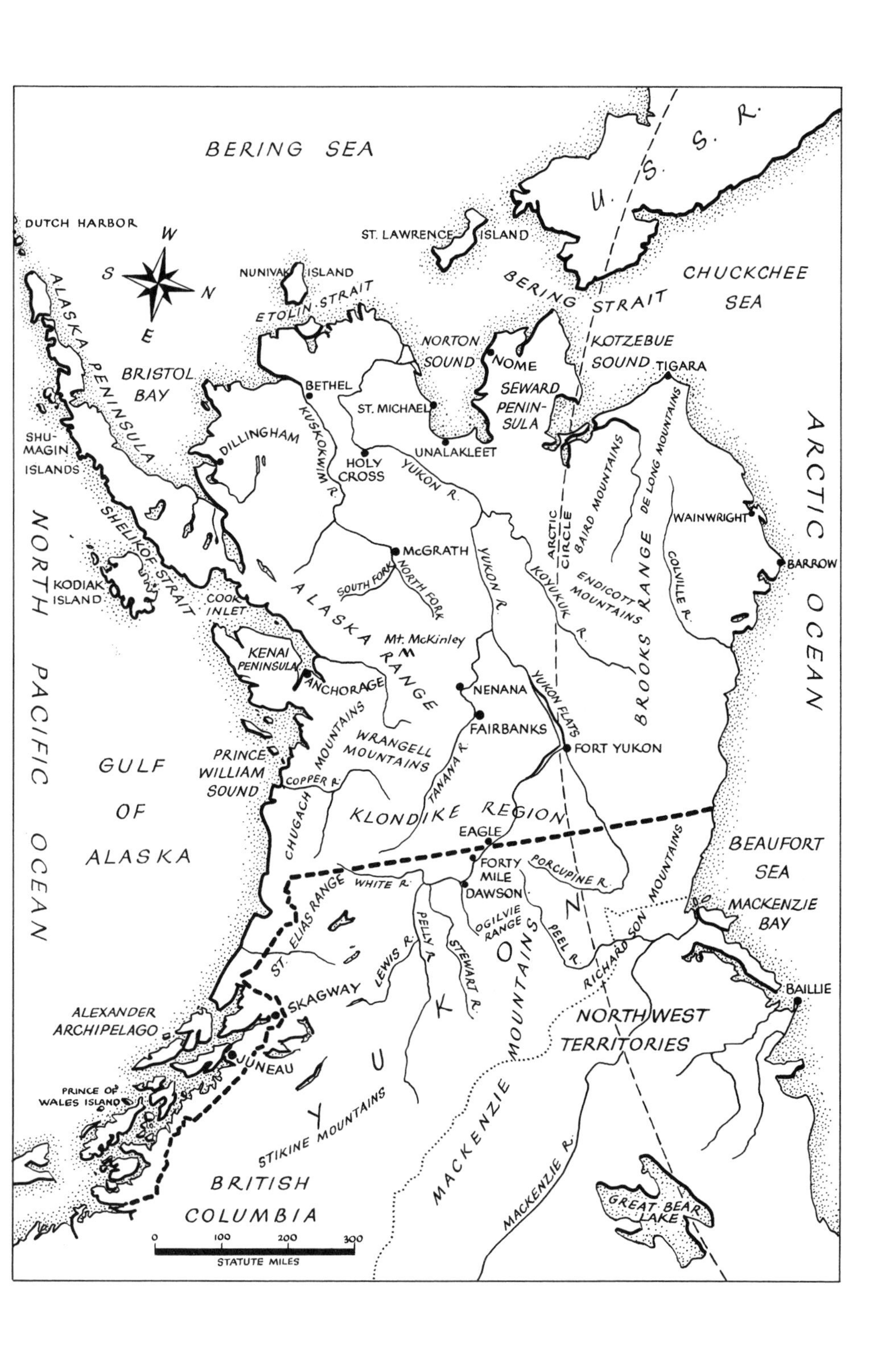

BERING SEA
U. S. S. R.
DUTCH HARBOR
ST. LAWRENCE ISLAND
NUNIVAK ISLAND
BERING STRAIT
CHUCKCHEE SEA
ETOLIN STRAIT
ALASKA PENINSULA
NORTON SOUND
NOME
KOTZEBUE SOUND
TIGARA
BRISTOL BAY
BETHEL
SEWARD PENINSULA
ST. MICHAEL
SHUMAGIN ISLANDS
DILLINGHAM
UNALAKLEET
HOLY CROSS
YUKON R.
KUSKOKWIM R.
BAIRD MOUNTAINS
DE LONG MOUNTAINS
ARCTIC OCEAN
ARCTIC CIRCLE
WAINWRIGHT
SHELIKOF STRAIT
McGRATH
BARROW
NORTH PACIFIC OCEAN
KODIAK ISLAND
SOUTH FORK
NORTH FORK
ENDICOTT MOUNTAINS
COLVILLE R.
COOK INLET
ALASKA RANGE
KOYUKUK R.
Mt. McKinley
KENAI PENINSULA
ANCHORAGE
NENANA
BROOKS RANGE
YUKON FLATS
FAIRBANKS
PRINCE WILLIAM SOUND
WRANGELL MOUNTAINS
FORT YUKON
GULF OF ALASKA
CHUGACH MOUNTAINS
COPPER R.
TANANA R.
KLONDIKE REGION
EAGLE
BEAUFORT SEA
FORTY MILE
PORCUPINE R.
DAWSON
WHITE R.
MACKENZIE BAY
ST. ELIAS RANGE
OGILVIE RANGE
PELLY R.
STEWART R.
PEEL R.
RICHARDSON MOUNTAINS
LEWIS R.
SKAGWAY
BAILLIE
ALEXANDER ARCHIPELAGO
NORTH WEST TERRITORIES
YUKON
JUNEAU
PRINCE OF WALES ISLAND
STIKINE MOUNTAINS
MACKENZIE MOUNTAINS
MACKENZIE R.
BRITISH COLUMBIA
GREAT BEAR LAKE
0
100
200
300
STATUTE MILES

Russian Big Diomede (left); American Little Diomede (right)

From the viewpoint of the United States, Alaska appears as a sort of doorstep leading from America to the North Pole neighborhood of nations: Norway, Sweden, Denmark, Finland, and—closest of all—Russia. The Aleutian Islands arise from the Pacific Ocean like a broken chain between Asia and America; they were used as stepping stones by the Japanese for their attempted invasion of Alaska in 1942. If there should be a fight anywhere in this neighborhood, Alaska is a place from which bombers could fly easily to any spot in the northern half of the world. It is because Alaska is so strategically located that General William Mitchell said, "Whoever controls Alaska controls the world."

Looking westward into Russia from America's Little Diomede village

Many Americans are surprised to learn that Russia is so near to the United States; they ordinarily think of Mexico on the south and Canada on the north as their only close neighbors. Actually, the Rio Grande River between the United States and Mexico is wider in places than the narrow Bering Strait which separates the United States from Russia at the Diomede Islands. These two tiny islands—less than three miles apart—lie about midway between Cape Prince of Wales, the westernmost part of America, and East Cape, the easternmost part of Russia. Between the two islands falls the International Boundary Line—which is also, at this point, the Iron Curtain between Russia and the United States—the only common frontier between the two countries.

A small group of Eskimos, a priest, and a schoolteacher and his wife are the only residents of America's Little Diomede village.

From here they can look across the narrow channel at Russia's Big Diomede Island. The Russian village on Big Diomede is hidden from view around the southern tip of the island. Little Diomede Eskimos were held prisoner there in 1949; they returned to their home island later with stories of cruel treatment by the Russian officers, and observations regarding the operation of the Russian radio on Big Diomede Island.

The boys and girls in the United States government school on Little Diomede use many of the same books to learn about geography, history, and government in our democracy that are used in schools everywhere in the United States. But only six miles away, at Big Diomede village, the boys and girls must learn to be Communists from books written and approved by Communist leaders.

Before the days of the Iron Curtain, Eskimo families from Russia visited their relatives every summer at Little Diomede Island and Cape Prince of Wales. They would cross the open water of Bering Strait in their big walrus-skin boats called "oomiaks." Each oomiak carried about twenty people, a few dogs, goods to be traded, and camping gear. This route from Asia to America by way of the Diomedes may have been followed thousands of years ago by the early people who came to the American continent from Asia.

The Russian Eskimos from Big Diomede Island were year-round visitors at the American Eskimo village of Little Diomede. In the winter they could easily walk across the sea ice between the islands. They came to visit relatives and to trade fine old fossil ivory for American wool yarn, pipes, and tobacco. There was always dancing and feasting—and of course the American Eskimos made return visits to the Russian village. But now the people dare not pass the Iron Curtain. No longer can American and Russian relatives and friends feast and dance and trade with one another. They must wait until worldwide peace dissolves the barrier. Then Americans and Russians can again be neighborly.

CHAPTER II

The Country

Alaska has thousands of miles of shoreline, which, in the south and southeast, zigzags into deep, ocean-filled valleys. These narrow inlets, or fiords, lie between the tops of steep mountain ridges that reach like long, crooked fingers to the sea. The peaks and ridges farthest out are entirely surrounded by water, making hundreds of mountainous islands.

Some of these islands, such as Baranof, Chichagof, and Admiralty are many miles in length and breadth. High mountains covered with dense forests rise from the narrow beaches of the mainland and the larger islands. Along the shores of the numerous inlets and channels are scattered mining and logging camps, salmon canneries, and lonely little towns. Tourists often stop at the Admiralty Island Game Reserve to photograph bears. Those who prefer to shoot their bears go farther west, to Kodiak Island, where many a big-game hunter comes every year, hoping to bag one of these huge brown creatures.

The hundreds of islands of southeastern Alaska shelter the inland waterways from the heavy storms of the North Pacific. These protected channels form the calm and scenic steamer lane known as the Inside Passage. This mountainous shoreline, with its

Mt. McKinley

inland passages, dense forests, glaciers, and fiords, is world famous for its beauty.

Farther westward, along the treeless Alaska Peninsula and the long bleak Aleutian Island chain, there is little to attract tourist travel. Landlubbers pray for good weather; for these are rough waters during the violent storms so common in this part of the world. Rocky headlands streaked with volcanic ash rise sharply from the sea.

Farther to the north the shorelines of the Bering Sea and the Arctic Ocean are low and flat and treeless. There are miles of swampy tide flats between the low headlands and capes. Here and

Mt. Katmai

there a range of hills reaches to the sea. Landing conditions along these shores are very difficult because of shallow waters and the absence of suitable docks. Dense fog hangs close to the water and the tundra lands for weeks at a time.

Alaska mountains are steep and high. The Rocky Mountains extend from the United States northwestward through Canada into Alaska. Here they form the Alaska Range of the Interior and the Brooks Range of the Arctic. Many of the mountain peaks rise to more than 10,000 feet. The most famous of these is Mt. McKinley, 20,320 feet high, the highest peak in North America.

The beauty of these snow-capped mountains is one of Alaska's

A glacier bed

chief attractions for tourists. The United States government has established a national park at the base of Mt. McKinley. The park is a stop-over point on the Alaska Railroad, and here the railroad operates a modern, comfortable hotel where one may spend a delightful vacation, enjoying the winter sports and sightseeing trips. Moose, bears, wolves, and other animals are protected by law in the park; here they roam wild, to the delight of nature-lovers and camera fans.

Some of Alaska's most beautiful mountains are active volcanoes. Not since Mt. Katmai "blew its top" in 1912 have there been any serious eruptions. But with nearly a hundred known volcanoes in

Tundra lands

Alaska there is seldom a time when one or more of them is not belching smoke, steam, and volcanic ash into the sky. At times this powdery ash falls like snow for days. For miles around, everything turns a dull gray color. The gritty powder hurts people's eyes, gets into their food, and creeps into every crack and crevice.

Earth tremors are common—much more common than thunderstorms in Alaska; for thunder and lightning are actually rare in this country. Boiling hot-springs, little cousins of the volcanoes, are found in many parts of the country. At Circle Hot Springs, in the Yukon Valley, and at Pilgrim Hot Springs, on the Seward Peninsula, buildings have been successfully heated with this natural hot-spring water.

Glaciers cover more than 20,000 square miles of Alaska's mountains. The largest ones are in the southern and eastern parts, where there are heavy snowfalls. The snow accumulates on the high mountains in the winter more rapidly than it can melt during the short cool summers. These great masses of snow gradually turn to ice, fill the valleys between the mountains, and slowly drain back into the sea as glaciers. At the sea they break off, leaving jagged walls of ice hundreds of feet high. Icebergs, some as big as city blocks, break away from the glaciers and float out to sea. When they drift into steamer lanes, they are dangerous to ships.

In addition to glaciers and snow and ice on the surface of Alaska, there are places where ice and frost extend—no one knows how far—below the surface. Much of the land of the Interior and the Arctic is permanently frozen beneath the thin layer of topsoil. People dig pits into this permanently frozen soil—or "permafrost," as it is called—to make deep-freezes for storing food. Large areas of permafrost, covered with muck and silt, form the tundra lands of the Yukon and Kuskokwim River deltas as well as the river deltas and tide flats of the Arctic.

In summer, pools, lakes, swamps, and sluggish streams cover the surface of the tundra. Only a few inches of the topsoil thaws. Moss, matted hummocks of swamp grass, clumps of willows, and colorful tundra flowers appear. The tundra pools, lakes, and streams are the breeding places of countless waterfowl—and mosquitoes. In winter the tundra is covered with drifted snow, the whiteness broken only by the brown tops of scraggly willows.

The rivers of Alaska are shallow, crooked, and hard to navigate. In summer the natives and traders travel from village to village in little motorboats. Small barges loaded with supplies for the winter spend weeks traveling from the sea coast to the trading posts along the rivers. In winter, dog teams follow the frozen rivers, taking

Frozen streams

many short cuts across the countless bends and loops, to shorten the trail.

The silted river valleys afford rich farmlands, the most famous of which is in the valley of the Matanuska. Small tracts of fertile soil are found nearly everywhere. Even north of the Arctic Circle little gardens are coaxed to yield a harvest of potatoes and cabbages and turnips. Southern Alaska offers all of these, plus huge strawberries and a profusion of sweet peas, pansies, gladiolas, and other garden flowers.

Spruce and hemlock, with a sprinkling of cedar, make up the valuable forests of the south and southeastern coasts. The sparse forests of the Interior consist of white spruce and Alaska birch, with scrub growth of alder and willow.

Almost before the snow melts in the spring there is hardly a spot in Alaska where flowers do not begin to grow. Violets, tiny orchids, "shooting-stars," iris, lupin, fireweed, and skunk cabbage —all these are common in southern and interior Alaska. Even the mossy Arctic tundra is color-splashed with flowers as the winter snow melts away. Delicious wild berries grow almost everywhere.

In southern Alaska the winters are warm, the summers cool— and it rains the year round. In the winter it is warmer in this part of Alaska than it is in Boston, New York, or Chicago. Here the heavy snows of winter are often washed away by rains before they melt. Even though the summers are cool, there are many days when youngsters can play out-of-doors in their sunsuits, or wade in the shallow water along a sandy beach. The ocean water, chilled by icebergs or streams of ice water from the glaciers, is usually too cold for swimming.

In the Interior the winters are long and cold. Snow comes early, in August or September. Within a few weeks most of the streams are frozen and will be ice-locked until May or June. By November there is enough snow to make good dog-team trails. Along the coast of the Bering Sea and the Arctic Ocean, winter is a cold, bleak period. Boats and barges must be hauled up onto the beach early in the fall or they will be crushed by the sea ice.

In the far north, the Arctic ice pack is seldom more than a few miles offshore. Even in midsummer it may drift against the beach and keep the annual supply boat from landing the supplies for the year. Then the worried people watch the ice night and day, hoping that the wind and tide will quickly move it out again so the supply boat can slip in and unload its cargo. They know that if the boat cannot leave the supplies, they will have a very hard time. Food and clothing, guns and ammunition for hunting, even Christmas presents to be exchanged later—all come on the supply boat when it makes its one stop for the year, usually in August. The ice pack

Cabin buried by midwinter snows

is often troublesome at the village of Barrow, which is only about a thousand miles from the North Pole. Here the shore is clear of ice for only a few weeks at the most during the summer months. It is hard to tell when the wind may change and the beach will again be locked tight in the grip of the sea ice.

During the long Arctic winter raging blizzards drive the snow into huge drifts on the lee side of every house. For months at a time it is never warmer than zero, and at times the temperature drops to seventy below zero! It is often too cold to hunt.

Most dreary of all is the continuous twilight of midwinter. North of the Arctic Circle there are a few weeks in midwinter during which the sun never rises, though on clear days it may appear as a dull glow on the horizon. But early in January it appears again and stays in sight a few minutes longer each day. By February there are many hours of sunlight on clear days, and by May or June there is enough light to read ordinary print at midnight. The birds are busy twenty-four hours a day. Boys and girls object to

The midnight sun photographed on the same film at fifteen-minute intervals from 10:30 p.m. to 1:30 a.m.

going to bed, because it isn't dark. The sun never drops below the horizon during a few weeks of midsummer. The sun sinks close to the horizon at midnight, then rises again, to continue the unbroken summer daylight.

CHAPTER III

The People

Little is known about what happened in Alaska before the arrival of the early explorers who kept written records. The native people of Alaska had no written language. They still have many folk stories and legends handed down from generation to generation by word of mouth, but these stories tell us little about the origin and development of the first people of Alaska.

However, archaeologists have carefully studied old tools, weapons, and other relics dug from the ancient villages of the early Alaskans. Their observations have yielded much information about the primitive homes, travels, and ways of life. Many scientists believe that the first people of Alaska came from Asia, from across the Bering Sea.

The first known visitors who left written records were the Russians. Vitus Bering, a Danish sea captain sailing for the Russian government, reported the discovery of Alaska in the year 1741. The Bering Sea is named for him. His discovery of America from the west occurred almost two hundred and fifty years after Columbus landed on San Salvador, from the east, in 1492, and a hundred and twenty-one years after the Pilgrims landed at Plymouth Rock in 1620. The first Fourth of July, in 1776, was celebrated only thirty-five years after Bering landed in Alaska.

Following Bering's discovery, the Russians made many fur-trading and hunting expeditions along the Bering Sea coast and the Aleutian Islands. In 1784 the first Russian colony was established at Three Saints Bay, on Kodiak Island. Other colonies followed, the most famous of which is Sitka, in southeastern Alaska—today one of the most important Alaskan towns. Many islands, mountains, and towns still have Russian names. There are still several Russian Orthodox Greek Catholic churches dotted along the coast, from St. Michael on the northwest coast, to Sitka in the southeast.

By the middle of the nineteenth century, explorations along the Alaska coast had been made by England, France, Spain, and the United States. The United States sent out the Kennicott Expedition in an early attempt to establish a telegraph line to Europe by way of Alaska. Kennicott's reports described the timber, fur, coal, and whaling resources of Alaska and suggested the possibility of gold in the country. The reports of these early explorers, as well as the world political situation at the time, led the United States, in 1867, to buy Alaska from Russia. The price was a little more than seven million dollars—about two cents an acre!

Only a few pioneers wandered into the country before the end of the century. Then gold was discovered. Thousands of men rushed to Alaska in hopes of becoming rich. Many returned disappointed—though some did become rich—and a few stayed in the country. Some of those who remained married Indian and Eskimo women and were among the pioneer families who started early villages and trading centers.

These pioneers were often called "Sourdoughs." They probably got this name from their favorite food, sourdough hot-cakes. They could not buy yeast, so they let the pancake batter sour slightly to make it light. Sourdough hot-cakes are a favorite food today, both in and out of Alaska. To one who has lived long in Alaska, and learned to love this great country, it is a true compliment to be called a "Sourdough."

Newcomers are called "Cheechakos," meaning persons untried

and inexperienced in the ways of the country. In general, everyone is considered a Cheechako until he has been in Alaska a year, or at least until he has seen the rivers freeze in the fall and break up again in the spring. In many ways the name has the same meaning as "tenderfoot," or "greenhorn"—terms often used in a friendly way to poke fun at a newcomer.

Many changes have taken place since the first explorers arrived. Schools, missions, and particularly the airplane and the radio have altered the way of living in Alaska. But approximately 35,000 natives—Indians, Eskimos, and Aleuts—still live in those parts of Alaska where they have always had their homes.

Three tribes of Indians—Tlingits, Haidas, and Tsimpseans—live in southeastern Alaska. The Tinneh tribes live in the valley of the Yukon River and its tributaries. They appear to be related to the Athabascans of Canada and the United States. The largest United States tribe, the Navajo of Arizona and New Mexico are part of this group, calling themselves Dineh.

In language, history, and custom the southeastern Alaskan Indians are most like the Indians of the northwest coast of the United States and of British Columbia. Since before the memory of man they have been the fishermen and seafarers of the northwest. These are the famous totem-pole Indians who carved monuments in cedar to honor their dead, to record their great events, or to shame their enemies.

Today the southeast Alaskan Indian differs little from his white fellow citizen in language and clothing, in the work he does, or in the way he lives. The days of the community houses, war canoes, potlatches, ceremonials, and totem poles are over, except for an occasional celebration or as a tourist attraction.

The Eskimos in Alaska live along the shores of the Bering Sea and the Arctic Ocean as well as on the tundra lands of the Kobuk River, the lower Yukon delta, and the Kuskokwim River basin. The largest town in the Eskimo country is Nome. Although half the population here is Eskimo, Nome is usually considered a white

An old Tlingit medicine man wearing an ancient spruce-root ceremonial hat, an iron collar from the early Russian occupation, and a shirt decorated with wampum, buttons, and beads

man's town. It is the business, shopping, and medical center of the northwest. In the Kuskokwim River area, Bethel is the business and transportation center. Larger villages—almost exclusively Eskimo—are Barrow, Wainwright, Kotzebue, and Unalakleet.

An Eskimo village. Sod-covered igloos and native huts, hard to see from the air, cluster around the schoolhouse. Other frame buildings may include trading posts and the missionary's house. This village has a reindeer packing plant (extreme right)

Eskimo villages are usually small, consisting sometimes of only three or four families. Larger villages are made up of a hundred or more families; in these communities there are usually one or two teachers, a trader, and often a missionary. The sod igloos, cabins, and shacks cluster around the schoolhouse and trading post. In summer the sandy beaches are littered with dories and kayaks, chained dogs and racks of drying fish.

It is often hard to tell which village or camp an Eskimo means when he speaks of home. He may be very much at home for a few weeks in the summer in a sod igloo or in a tent where there is good salmon-fishing and berry-picking. Also he may have a summer camp on a beach which will be his home while he is seal-hunting. However, the Eskimos usually build their best igloos in the places where they spend the long winter months, and if possible they choose a village where there is a school for the children. This village becomes their main home.

The Aleuts are at home on the Alaska Peninsula and the Aleutian Islands. These people are the mixed-blood descendants of the Eskimos who lived on these islands and of the Russians who conquered and abused them. The history of the Aleuts is very sad. About two hundred years ago they were enslaved by the early Russian hunters who came to Alaska in search of sea otter and other furs. It was common for small bands of Russian hunters to enter a village and capture the women as hostages and slaves. Then they would force the Aleut men to hunt for fur with which to buy back their wives and families. All too often the promises to return the women were broken. The Aleut fur-hunters were killed and the women as well as the furs were carried away. Enraged by such treatment, the Aleuts revolted against the Russians in 1762, killing many of the hunters and destroying their ships. But the Aleuts' spears and arrows were no match for Russian gunpowder and brutality, and the Aleuts who survived were forced into submission.

In 1942, shortly after the Pearl Harbor incident, the Japanese attacked the Aleuts at Attu and Atka as an early step in their attempted invasion of the United States by way of Alaska. The Attu Aleuts who were not killed—men, women, and children—were held as prisoners in Japan for many months, where several of them died. About a year after V-J Day those who were still alive were brought back to Alaska. A few of them now live in Atka village. Attu village was completely destroyed in a battle between United States forces and the Japanese and has never been rebuilt.

Because of the long years of Russian influence, the Aleut language of today is a curious mixture of the original Aleut with many Russian words. Most of the Aleuts are members of the Russian Orthodox Greek Catholic Church. Today, as fishermen, seamen, cannery workers, laborers, and homemakers, these westernmost of Uncle Sam's citizens are again happy in their clean little cottages.

In addition to approximately 40,000 Eskimos, Indians, and

Aleuts, there are about 175,000 white persons residing in the Territory. When one considers that Alaska covers roughly half a million square miles, it is obvious that a good part of the Territory is sparsely populated. In fact, there are about two and a half square miles per person, in comparison with a States average of fifty-four people per square mile. True, Alaska gives much space to glaciers, tundra land, and steep, snow-covered mountains that defy habitation. However, she is generous with resources that can be developed; in addition to fisheries, forests, farmlands, gold, and fur, there is reason to believe that there are other resources such as oil and certain minerals waiting to be utilized.

One might guess that in this still wild country most people would be hunters and trappers. Actually, trappers are among the smallest occupational groups in the Territory. With the changes so rapidly taking place in Alaska there has been a great influx of construction workers. Bulldozer and crane operators, carpenters, welders, blacksmiths, machinists, and hundreds of other skilled and unskilled workers are building roads, bridges, airfields, and military and naval installations. The fast-growing cities also employ construction workers for hotels, apartment houses, private homes, and public buildings. In Alaskan cities, too, many people work, as they do in cities in the States, in stores, restaurants, bars, hotels, laundries, public-utilities companies, and for numerous other employers.

There are many fishermen and cannery workers, as well as workers in cold-storage plants, on public docks, and with commercial transportation companies. By using modern boats and gear, and up-to-date methods of canning and freezing fish, they bring Alaska's salmon, halibut, crabs, shrimps, and clams to the world's markets. Another rapidly increasing group of workers is employed by the pulp mills.

Federal employees in Alaska carry on the work of several government departments, including the United States Public Health Service, the Forest Service, the Fish and Wildlife Service, and the

A gold dredge

Bureau of Indian Affairs. United States government surveyors, geologists, engineers, and many skilled technicians are found throughout the Territory. There are forest rangers, who patrol in sturdy little boats instead of on horseback as they do in the States—for they must cruise the waters of the Tongass and Chugach National Forests. Game wardens often pilot their own planes to lonely streams and traplines to enforce the laws and protect the fish, game, and fur animals. Other federal employees in Alaska include schoolteachers for the Bureau of Indian Affairs who teach Eskimos, Indians, and Aleuts; doctors and nurses in outlying hospitals; traveling public-health nurses in certain areas; lighthouse-keepers; and employees of the Alaska Railroad.

The number of miners is small. The days of the lonely mosquito-ridden prospector with his gold pan are nearly over. Modern prospecting requires expensive machinery for drilling test holes and

Ground crew servicing a plane

analyzing ore samples. Once a deposit of gold or platinum or other precious metal is located, a few technicians and miners can operate the hydraulic jets and huge dredges that glean the precious metal from thousands of tons of gravel.

Many workers are required to keep Alaska's planes in the air. In addition to the pilots, navigators, radio operators, stewardesses, and flight mechanics who make up the plane crews, and outnumbering them by far, are the ground crews. Even the bush pilot who has no plane crew must have some ground service. The unseen man who keeps the motors and generators humming to light a lonely airport, the operator in a snowbound radio beam station, and the man who drives the snowplow in a freezing wind to clear a runway wear no wings; these men are seldom seen, but they add their bit to Alaska's record for safe flying.

No class of workers or pioneers has done more than the Alaskan bush pilot to break down the barriers of distance and climate on the frontier. Even today, many a remote village and mining camp has no airfield suitable for a large plane. Only the bush pilot will undertake a landing on a small tundra lake, or drop over a mountain onto a river bar to deliver supplies or to bring out a sick or injured person. Many Eskimo and Indian communities, and a host of traders, trappers, miners, and fishermen, depend on the service of the bush pilot.

It would be impossible to say who has contributed most toward making Alaska the great country it is today. The Indians, Eskimos, and Aleuts have given freely of their knowledge of the country. They helped the early pioneers to learn to live—how to secure food, clothing, and shelter in a strange, wild country. Businessmen with faith in the possibilities of developing Alaska's resources have generously invested and risked capital in the large mining, fishing, lumber, and pulp industries, all of which are essential to the economic growth and development of Alaska—America's giant in the north.

Another group of people who have given the highest kind of public service are the many teachers, missionaries, and nurses, who have willingly given up their accustomed comforts, conveniences, and companionships to live and work in the small villages of Alaska. Other humanitarian and religious leaders have established homes and institutions, with educational programs for homeless children. All these people have done much to promote

Sig Wien, "king" of the bush pilots

the physical, educational, spiritual, and economic welfare of the people of Alaska, and to help them to become a vital part of our American way of life.

Of course there have been some newcomers who found disappointment and experienced failure in Alaska. Many could not endure the physical discomfort and hardships. Some could not

A beautiful University of Alaska coed, the mixed-blood daughter of a pioneer family

adjust happily to living with a different people. Then, too, there have been selfish people who came to Alaska with only one purpose—to exploit the resources and people of Alaska, to make their fortunes and get out of the country as soon as possible. Stories are told of ruthless traders, trappers, fur-buyers, miners, fishermen, and others who came to Alaska with nothing, but became wealthy in only a few years at the expense of the good people who befriended them.

Unfortunately, even the sympathetic white man unwittingly brought certain injuries to this new country. Diseases which had long been common to the white man but were new to Alaska caused suffering and death for many thousands of native people. Liquor, too, proved to be one of the greatest evils introduced by the newcomers.

Since the coming of the white man, several generations of mixed-blood children have been born. There are many fine mixed-blood families in which happy youngsters show the good qualities they have inherited from their white and native parents. Many of these children have grown up to become leaders in village life—businessmen, nurses, aviators, teachers, ministers, and legislators.

These new generations of Alaskans are living harmoniously side by side with their white and native neighbors. Race discrimination is gradually fading. The ways of living and the different races of people are merging into well-organized communities, accepting fully the responsibilities of citizenship.

The majority of Alaskans are deeply concerned with the disadvantages of their territorial status. As citizens of a territory Alaskans do not have the right to vote in presidential elections or to elect their own governor—nor do they have a voting representative in Congress. The governor of the Territory is appointed by the President of the United States. The people of the Territory elect a delegate to Congress who may speak on behalf of the Territory but does not have the right to vote.

In December 1955, a convention of fifty-five delegates, men and women representing all of Alaska, met at the University of Alaska to draft a state constitution, or plan of government. They agreed on a constitution on February 5, 1956, and about six weeks later the people of Alaska voted their approval of it. Now it remains only for Congress to take action in order that Alaska may become a state—one of the United States of America.

CHAPTER IV

Life in a Small Coastal Village

Small fishing and cannery villages dot the coastlines of the mainland and the larger islands all the way from southeast Alaska to the Alaska Peninsula. There are also a few at the head of Bristol Bay, where the Nushagak and Kvichak Rivers empty into the Bering Sea. These villages are the homes of the salmon-fishermen and cannery workers. In fact, it is usually the presence of the salmon that has determined the location of the villages.

For longer than anyone knows, the salmon have followed certain ocean paths each year. They come back to the very same streams where they were hatched to spawn and die. Over many years the fishermen have learned that fishing is usually best at certain points along the ocean trails of the salmon. At these places the canneries have been built and the nearby villages have grown up. The salmon were there first; the villages and canneries followed.

Salmon are summer visitors only. Conservation laws allow only a short summer season during which these fish may be taken for commercial purposes. So from October until May the fishing boats are little used. The owners live in the village cottages and visit the boats daily during the winter to keep them pumped dry and to make sure that they do not break their moorings and drift away.

Metlakatla, a large and prosperous fishing village

In spring each man spends many days getting his boat and fishing gear in perfect condition for the busy days of the salmon run.

Many fishermen own the boats they operate. The larger boats equipped with nets or seines are called "seiners." An owner may have to pay as much as fifty thousand dollars for his seiner with all the necessary gear.

Smaller fishing boats with two to four long poles, each trailing a line with several hooks on it, are called "trollers." A good troller costs ten thousand dollars or more. Owners may be in debt for many years before they can catch enough salmon to pay off the mortgages on their boats. At the same time, of course, they must take care of their families and buy new fishing gear as it is needed. Lines and nets wear out surprisingly fast; often they are lost or badly damaged. Thousands of dollars must be spent on seines alone.

A troller

Fishermen who are unable to buy boats for themselves work as crew members on the boats of the more prosperous fishermen. Their wages are paid as part of the boat's earnings, divided into shares.

Owners and crew members must know how to do many things to keep boats, engines, and fishing gear in good condition. They must be competent at painting, calking, overhauling engines, and doing numerous repair jobs to keep the boats in perfect running order. They must be skillful in handling the nets and lines when there are heavy runs of fish. They must know how to "tan" the nets, or treat them with chemicals to preserve them. They often store the nets in the dry lofts of the cannery buildings.

There are many different ways of seining salmon. One of the most common is purse-seining. On a typical seining trip the fishermen will shout with excitement when a school of salmon is sighted. The crew "pays out" the seine over the stern as the seine boat

Mending a fishing net

chug-chugs slowly along, laying the net in a circle several hundred feet across, around the fish.

In the water, the web of the seine hangs straight down from the "float line." This is a small rope on which are strung huge beads of cork or wood that float the upper edge of the net at the surface of the water. The lower edge of the net is lashed to a line weighted with heavy beads of lead, each about an inch in length. This line is called the "lead line," and it sinks the lower edge of the net about eight feet below the float line. Now the seine forms a huge fence or corral around the school of salmon. A few inches below the lead line hang the purse rings, through which the purse line runs like a giant drawstring, to close, or "purse," the seine. This kind of seine is named after the old-fashioned money purse that is closed with a drawstring.

Once inside the seine fence, frightened fish swim madly in all directions, but when the bottom of the purse has been closed, they cannot escape. All the fishermen smile as the seine is pulled alongside the boat and they can see that it is full of large, fine fish. "A good haul!" yells the skipper. Leaping, splashing fish are dipped from the seine into the hold of the boat with a dipper-shaped brailing net, which is hoisted by power from the boat's engine. The bottom of the net opens, and the thrashing, silvery fish flop and slide into the well-iced hold.

When the hold is full, or at least every twenty-four hours, the seiner must deliver the fish to a cannery or to a fish-buyer's boat. The trip to the cannery may take several hours or even overnight. On the way, one of the fishermen, who is also cook for the seiner crew, goes to the tiny galley and prepares a big meal—pork chops, perhaps, and mashed potatoes and bread and butter, with canned fruit and doughnuts for dessert. Big mugs of black coffee are filled again and again. All the men are very hungry, as no one has dared to take time to eat while the fishing has been good. After eating, the men rest, sleep, and take their turns at steering the boat until they arrive at the cannery.

If several boats are coming into the cannery at once to unload, each must await its turn. But no one cares. During the salmon-fishing season the daylight lasts almost all night long, and good fishing means bigger shares for everybody and a better winter ahead, for each of the crew gets a percentage of the boat's earnings, and if the boat has a good season the wages are generous. There may be enough money for extra clothing, more toys for the children, and perhaps even a new washing machine. When fishing is good many air-castles are built.

Soon it's time to unload. The seiner is tied up alongside the cannery unloading float and the fish are pitched out one at a time

Dipping fish from a seine into the hold of a boat

with a tool called a "pue," which is like a single-tined pitchfork. The men are very careful to stick the pue into the head of each fish so that the sharp steel tine will not damage any of the fine firm flesh that will soon be in cans and ready for the markets of the

A pair of salmon from Daddy's catch

world. The fish are pitched onto a conveyer belt which carries them high above the dock to the cannery fish house.

Then the big, silver-colored salmon drop from the conveyer into huge white-painted bins. Next they slip, head first, into a machine known as an "Iron Chink" because it was designed to do the work for which Chinese labor was originally employed. This machine guts and cleans the fish and in a few moments the delicious meat is firmly packed into cans and ready for cooking. Thousands of cans at a time, in special racks, are wheeled along narrow tracks into tunnel-like pressure cookers and are cooked at high temperatures.

Boys and girls watch for their fathers' boats from the cannery dock. As soon as the boat ties up, they jump aboard. They raid the galley for leftover doughnuts and cookies, and, like pirates, seize the special fish saved for home use. Among Alaskans salmon is a favorite food—fresh, smoked, dried, or canned.

Near the canneries small sharks gather to eat the waste from the fish butchering. The sharks are fighting mad when they come in on the hooks, and their sharp teeth could easily snap off unwary fingers. Boys under sixteen—too young to work in the cannery—often make money by catching these sharks and collecting the livers, which are frozen and sold to the manufacturers of vitamin pills.

Many families take a large part of their food—halibut, red snapper, crabs, shrimps, and clams—direct from the sea. The herring roe, or eggs, which we often see in the markets as caviar is a special delicacy, even to Alaskans. In the spring, spruce branches are placed in the shallow water where the herring will come to lay their eggs; soon the branches are covered with white masses of eggs. They are quickly cooked when dipped, branch and all, into boiling water; then they are eaten right from the branch.

But Alaska coastal villages do not depend entirely upon the sea for food. In small gardens quick-growing vegetables may be raised. It is important to choose varieties that will grow and ripen during the short cool summer. Potatoes, carrots, turnips, cabbage, and peas are favorite crops. Strawberries and raspberries grow wild or in gardens. Late-summer trips to the woods are made for wild blueberries, salmonberries, and currants. But a berry-picker must

A boy taking livers from his catch of small sharks

be cautious—bears are good berry-pickers too, and it would be very dangerous to startle a mother bear with cubs!

In addition to the garden vegetables and berries, there are many wild greens to be picked and preserved for later use. A slender green plant called "goose tongue" grows in the shallow water at the head of inlets where fresh-water streams flow into the sea. This

Playing outdoors in rain clothing

is prepared and served like spinach. Seaweed may be gathered from the rocks at low tide. Dried, it may be cooked with meat or eaten raw, so that its fine salty flavor may be fully enjoyed.

During the hunting seasons permitted by the Game Commission deer are shot in the forest. At times, imported beef, pork, and lamb may be bought at the village stores by a few people who can afford the very high prices of this kind of meat. Wild ducks and geese are plentiful, in season, all along the coast.

Since Alaska grows no grain, and no fruits other than berries, stores must carry large stocks of imported flour, cereal, sugar, and canned fruits and vegetables.

In coastal villages, almost all clothing is imported from the States. Stores carry large stocks of dress goods, ready-to-wear clothing, and heavy woolen pants, shirts, and underwear for outdoor work. Fishermen, seamen, and loggers need raincoats and heavy rubber boots. Work never stops because of rain. Everyone—children as well as grown-ups—has plenty of rain clothing.

Children in the southern part of Alaska wear the same kinds of garments to school that are worn by boys and girls in the States. In spite of rainy weather and washday troubles in drying clothes, little girls come to school in fresh starched dresses.

The store is a center of community life in the smaller towns and villages. The storekeeper is frequently the postmaster since store and postoffice are often in the same building. Here everyone gathers to wait for the mail as soon as the mail boat or the mail plane comes in. Often big packages are arriving, because many things are bought from mail-order companies in the States. Washing machines, furniture, and clothing are usually purchased in this way. It is in these stores that the men and women, as well as the boys and girls, spend a good part of the money they earn in the canneries, on the fish boats, or in other ways.

The village cooperative store is a good place to buy because the profits from this enterprise are divided among the people who own it. The more the villagers trade at their own co-op, the more money there will be to divide. To encourage trade at home, the manager of the village cooperative store keeps prices as low as possible, usually lower than those in the larger-town stores or in privately owned trading posts.

However, at the end of the fishing and canning season, when the people get their pay, nearly everyone goes to the nearest town

A village co-op

for special shopping and just for fun. Several families with their friends and relatives take the trip together on one seine boat. The fishing gear is removed and put away for the winter; the boat is cleaned and the engine checked. Then, with plenty of food for everyone, and plenty of fuel or Diesel oil for the engine, the party is off, for all the world like a big family on a picnic.

The trip may take more than a day, but if the weather is fine the boat travels day and night, the men and older boys taking turns at steering. There are many good things to eat, and everyone has a good time. The older boys and girls are kept busy watching toddlers to keep them from falling overboard or from getting too close to the engine or galley stove.

If the boat runs into a storm everyone must huddle in the tiny galley or crowd into the few bunks. A few of the passengers may get seasick. The captain is likely to be worried, and he sends everybody but his helpers out of the pilothouse. Full attention must be given to steering the boat, to operating the engine, and to keeping a sharp lookout for reefs and other dangers. Flashing signals from government lighthouses are welcome navigation aids.

When the party finally reaches town, everyone is very busy. The men buy special tools and parts for their boats and engines. The women buy coats and shoes and perhaps a few small pieces of furniture. There are candy and gum and ice cream, dolls and toy wagons, and new boots and shoes and sweaters for the children. The girls will get new cloth coats to wear to school, novelty skirts, and perhaps scarves, earrings, and bright-colored berets. The boys will be happy with overalls or dungarees, with bright belts. The storekeepers in the towns are always glad to see these shoppers from the outlying villages. They give the children small presents of candy, soft drinks, balloons, and souvenirs.

At the end of the long day of shopping there is just time to see a movie before the passengers must return to the boat. Finally all are aboard—dead tired—and they are homeward bound. With the exception of the faithful crewmen, who awaken one another to take turns operating the boat, everyone sleeps most of the way home. If good weather holds, the boat chugs steadily onward through a calm sea lane, marked by flashing lighthouses on either side.

Back home again in the village there is much to talk about. The new clothes must be shown off and the story of the movie told in detail to those who could not go on the trip. If someone has bought a radio, everyone must hear it as soon as possible. There is a great deal of fun trying out the new shop tools, kitchen gadgets, and the mechanical toys!

But there is still a lot of shopping to be done at the village store, to get ready for school and the colder weather ahead. The women buy yards and yards of bright print cloth to make attractive school dresses for the girls. The boys shop for shirts and warm jackets and caps with fur-lined earflaps. The men buy rifle and shotgun shells for the fall hunting season.

When the fall fishing season is over and the shopping is finished, the houses must be made snug and warm for the winter weather ahead. The high cost of building materials, combined with heavy rainfall and strong winds, make building and upkeep very costly and difficult. However, there are many comfortable modern homes in these coastal villages. Such a home may be a cozy two-room log cabin, common in the small towns, or a frame house with several rooms, usually found in the larger centers. A few of the well-to-do families have their own light plants and pumps for running water, just as do many people in the rural areas in the States.

In some villages it has been possible to build small dams so that each village has its own water supply. Water may be piped to a few homes, but more often it is piped to two or three centrally located hydrants. From these hydrants each family carries its supply in buckets. Other villages depend on nearby lakes or streams for their water.

Much fuel is needed, particularly during the dark and rainy winter days. Nearly everyone burns wood, which is plentiful but hard to make ready for use. Logs are floated to the beach in front of the village and cut into blocks with two-man cross-cut saws; the blocks are carried home and split into firewood. Coal is rarely used, because it must be shipped in from the States or from one of the few Alaska coal mines and is therefore very expensive.

After repairing the houses and securing a supply of fuel the villagers settle down for the winter. They are happy to return to a regular routine after all the strenuous fishing days, the long irregular shifts at the canneries, the haphazard meals and frequent lack of supervision and care for the small children. Now they have more time for family life and community affairs.

Now the children are eager to return to the village schools, which are much like small rural schools in the States. Some of the schools are provided by the United States Bureau of Indian Affairs; others are maintained by the Territory of Alaska. As the communities become better developed they organize their own school districts. Many of the teachers are young Indian men and women who have gone away to college for their training as teachers. In these village schools almost every boy and girl will finish the sixth or seventh grade. Those who want to go on to junior high school and high school, or to vocational schools, must arrange to live in one of the larger towns where high-school work is offered, or to attend one of the boarding schools, such as Pius X Mission School at Skagway, Sheldon Jackson School at Sitka, or Mt. Edgecumbe Federal Vocational School.

The ordinary business of the village is carried on by an elected chief, or mayor, and a small council. Matters of great importance are settled in general community meetings in which every adult has a voice and a vote. There are no policemen in the villages. The council may hire one of the local men as a town watchman, and it may also fine people for petty misdemeanors. But for serious crimes the village must depend on United States marshals who are called in from the larger towns. Criminals are tried in the United States Commissioners' Courts or in the District Courts. Those who are sentenced to jail for long terms are sent to the penitentiary in the State of Washington.

An Alaskan village usually has no organized fire department. In case of fire, everyone helps. Firefighting equipment is meager—usually only a few hand-operated fire extinguishers. Many homes burn every year. Great care is taken around the school and cannery buildings, for once a fire gets a good start, there is little chance of saving any part of them.

Hospitals, doctors, and dentists are available only in the large towns, such as Ketchikan, Juneau, Sitka, Anchorage, and Unalaska. In some villages there may be a resident or traveling public-health nurse. In a school operated by the Bureau of Indian Affairs there

The village chief, or mayor

is usually a small clinic where first-aid supplies and simple remedies are available. In case of serious illness or injury it is necessary to send for a plane to get the patient to a doctor or a hospital. For such emergencies and for other business almost every village has a radiophone operated by the teacher, trader, or missionary.

Almost every village has a church. Missionaries from the Baptist, Presbyterian, Episcopal, Roman Catholic, and other churches have established themselves throughout Alaska. Long before Alaska was bought from the Russians, the Russian Church had become widely established throughout the coastal areas. This church still greatly influences the lives of many people. In many homes the Russian Church votive lights burn on family shrines.

Southeast Alaska Indians are famous for their totem poles and

A simple cabin as a place of worship

the stories they tell of traditional beliefs and historical events. Remains of many of the old poles still exist. New copies of many have been made and placed in suitable settings or special parks. The killer-whale, bear, raven, frog, beaver, wolf, and other animals, as well as birds and various imaginary creatures, were carved as totemic figures. They represented different tribes and clans of people, even individuals, in various relationships to one another. Today there are very few of the skilled old carvers left. This kind of record is a thing of the past.

Totem poles are of several kinds. Commemorative poles were sometimes carved to record important events. The Seward pole, carved by a Tlingit chief in 1868, commemorates Secretary of State Seward's visit to Alaska. A likeness of Abraham Lincoln was

A wood carver making a totem pole

carved in 1867 to remind the United States government that the Tlingits were not accorded citizenship when the United States bought Alaska from the Russians. (All Indians now have citizenship.) Totem poles called "house poles" not only supported the

Carving a paddle

roof beams of the houses but recorded legends and events about the various families living in them.

The famous totem poles are not the only products of the Alaskan native's skill in the use of tools. His very livelihood depends on his ability to build and repair much of his fishing and hunting equipment. There are seldom carpenters or blacksmiths or mechanics in Alaskan villages. So many things must be homemade that most villages have community shops. A large schoolroom, the community store, or just an empty building heated by a wood-burning stove—any warm place where men may gather to share tools and visit while they work—may serve as a shop. Here a man may build a coffin, repair his boat, or make kitchen shelves for his wife.

An orphaned hair-seal pup

In general, life in these coastal villages is very pleasant. There are many things to do just for pleasure, such as fishing in the nearby streams and flying kites on clear, windy days. It's pleasant to linger on the village dock, where someone is sure to be tinkering with his boat—and there are always the squawking, squabbling sea gulls to watch. When it's warm enough, children sprawl on their tummies at the edge of the dock, to watch the small fish and umbrella-shaped jellyfish.

Once in a while someone rescues a baby seal from a fisherman's net. Then those who like animals really have fun for hours and hours. Baby seals love to be petted, and quickly learn to drink canned milk from a nursing bottle. These babies often stay with their human friends until they are nearly full-grown. Eventually, however, the call of the sea and the yearning for the herd win out, and they quietly swim away without even a farewell wave of a flipper!

CHAPTER V

With the Eskimos

In the land of the Eskimos, houses must be snug and warm, and made from materials close at hand. Many people believe that all Eskimos build igloos of blocks of ice and snow, similar to those built in Greenland, northwestern Canada, and other parts of the Arctic. This is not true in Alaska. Walls of snow are sometimes built as windbreaks to keep drifts from obstructing the doors of the houses. Large blocks of snow and ice are cut and stood on edge to shelter a person when he must sit for many hours fishing at a hole in the ice. In the same way seal-hunters often protect themselves where they must wait for the seals to surface in an open stretch of water. Fences at reindeer corrals may be patched with snow blocks, but snow and ice are rarely if ever used as building materials for an Alaskan home.

Alaskan igloos are usually constructed of rectangular chunks of sod, carefully cut from the tough, grassy tundra. These igloos are similar to the sod houses built by the early pioneers on the prairies in the West. Partly underground, the igloo is ordinarily a single room, reached through a long, low tunnel. Hunting and fishing equipment, frozen meat, driftwood, and blubber for fuel are stored in this tunnel, and sometimes a favored mother dog is allowed to

Sod igloo

have her pups in this sheltered entry. Whale bones, especially the large ribs, and driftwood are used to make the frame of the house. Sometimes when fuel is very scarce the family has to cut away this driftwood from the inside and burn it during the winter. Then, when spring comes, the sod thaws and the whole house tumbles in. The family moves out into a tent for the summer, and a new igloo must be built before fall. Even if the frame is not cut away, the sods must be replaced every summer. In spring, melting snow leaks through the roof, and sometimes the mud on the floor is several inches deep.

Almost everything at hand is made to serve some purpose in building a home. On Little Diomede Island, where neither sod nor logs are available, the houses are dug out of the side of a rocky slope. Layers of rocks, chinked with grass and moss, are used for parts of the walls. Walrus skins that have worn too thin to be of further use on the oomiaks—the large, hide-covered boats used for whaling and many other purposes—are used for roof covering. Scrapwood and crates thrown overboard from the annual supply ship, seal gut, driftwood, kerosene cans, oil drums—all are used as building materials. Some of the worst houses in certain villages are constructed from scrap lumber, canvas, cardboard cartons, and anything else that is found on the beach. Well-built sod igloos are much more comfortable and much safer than are such shacks.

Along the Arctic coast people are seldom so fortunate as to find enough driftwood for cabins. Usually this wood must be used for fuel. It is only in the inland villages, where small trees grow, that cabins are common. The Eskimo groups in the upper valley regions of the Kuskokwim River—also the Kobuk and Noatak Rivers, farther north—often have snug little log cabins. But for those who live in the larger, treeless villages along the coast, sod igloos are the most satisfactory and inexpensive kind of homes.

A well-built igloo is covered with tightly packed sod, with only a couple of holes left for the wooden ventilator and a simple chimney. Windows of seal gut are placed in the roof, as high as possible above the snow level. A fence around the window keeps people and stray dogs from falling through the gut-covered opening when the snow is drifted high and pathways run over the houses. The people tell stories of hungry polar bears who sometimes come into the village and try to dig into the igloos through the windows. The ventilators and stovepipes are often the only parts of the houses visible when the entire village becomes a big snowdrift. Then even the seal-gut windows are buried, and the men must very carefully scrape away the heavy snow to keep the windows from breaking under the weight.

When the winter blizzards bury the village, each family must dig a tunnel to get out of its igloo. The first people to emerge look for their neighbors to be sure that no one is trapped under the snow. Doors must be hinged so they will swing inward; otherwise a person would be locked in by the mass of snow at the entrance.

Lack of building materials and scarcity of fuel force several

Window of seal-gut in a roof

families to live together. Ten or more persons of all ages often crowd together into a small one-room igloo. Disease spreads rapidly in these overcrowded homes. Poor housing is one reason for the prevalence of tuberculosis among Eskimos.

Even though the homes are small, it is very difficult to keep warm in the Arctic climate. It may take several days to gather a little pile of twigs from the scrub willows and alders. In the few villages where there is driftwood on the beaches, it is cold, hard work to find these pieces, dig them out of the snow, and drag them home. Occasionally walrus or whale blubber is burned in tiny stoves made of empty oil tins; but usually these fats must be used for food.

The old-fashioned seal-oil lamp requires very little blubber for

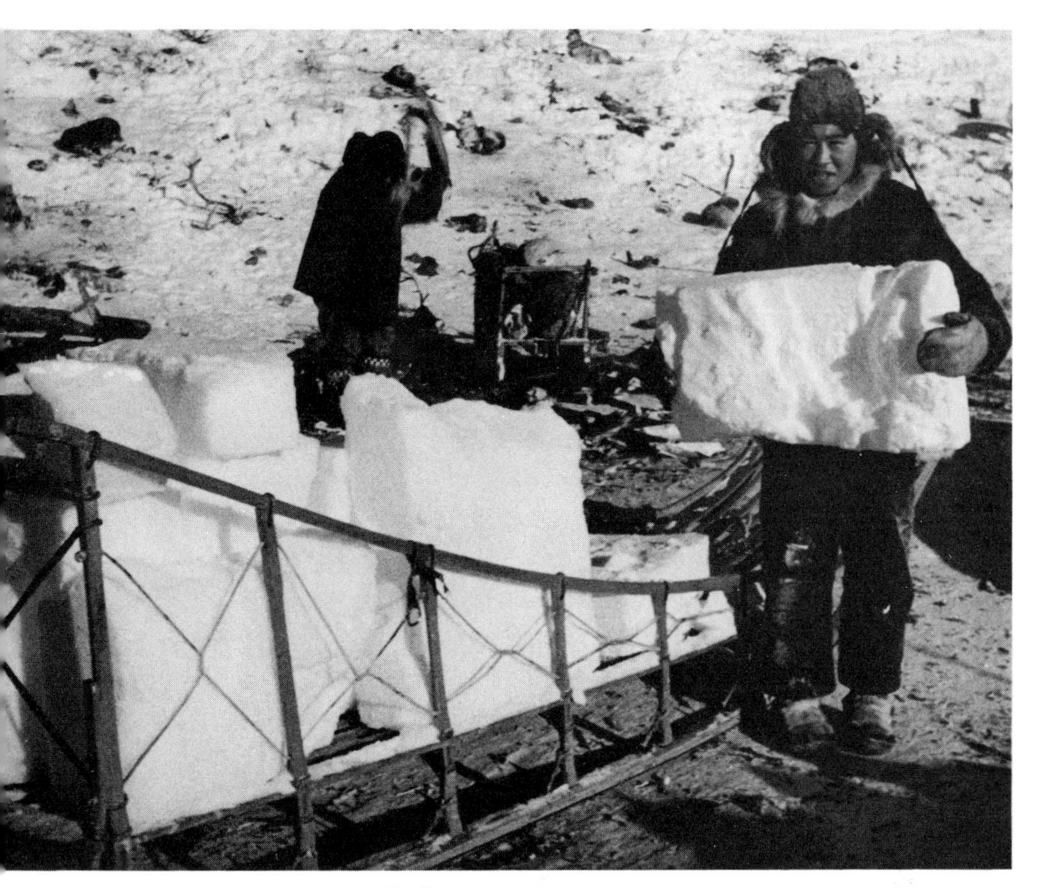

Hauling snow for water

fuel, and it gives a clear hot flame for light and cooking. For these reasons it is still used in many Eskimo homes. Families who can afford to buy kerosene for fuel oil use Primus stoves. Hunters often take these small stoves with them when traveling by dog team, especially in parts of the country where there is little or no wood.

A few fortunate villages such as Wainwright, Barrow, and Unalakleet have nearby outcroppings of low-grade coal, small quantities of which are mined by hand and hauled home either by dog team or by boat.

Water cannot be piped from lakes or streams because of the freezing temperatures, and wells cannot be dug in the frozen ground. A barrel of melting ice or snow is the only water supply for many homes. Clean snow or ice from lakes must be hauled into the village by dog team. Several sledloads of snow are needed to make a single tub of water. Clean clothes and clean bodies are hard-won luxuries. Because of little water and forever frozen ground, modern plumbing or even pits for sewage disposal are impossible. Sewage and garbage from the slop cans in the houses are simply thrown out the doors, or at best dumped on the beach. Even the most modern facilities in the Arctic are seldom more than wash basins and tubs to hold water heated on the stove, and chemical toilets. Doctors and engineers are working together, trying to find safe, convenient ways of disposing of wastes and other ways of improving sanitation and housing conditions in these villages.

Inside these little, crowded homes furnishings must be simple and few. Tiny stoves made of discarded five-gallon oil cans, small water barrels, and a few pots and pans are among the essential items. Beds are built like bunks or wide shelves; more often reindeer-skin sleeping bags are opened out on the floor at night and rolled into a corner by day. Simple meals are served in a few dishes on a low table or on the floor.

For the Eskimo, getting food means hunting and fishing and berry-picking. Fathers and mothers and children all help with food-gathering at one time or another.

Long before the Eskimo had the white man's guns and cartridges and steel traps, he was able to hunt and kill animals for food and clothing. Some of the clever tools and weapons designed by these skillful hunters are displayed in museums in Alaska, in the States, and elsewhere. Even today, for certain kinds of hunting the Eskimo weapons are better than the white man's expensive rifle and ammunition. Many times it is better to use the new and the old equipment together. For example, a seal shot with a modern rifle is pulled to the edge of the ice floe with an old-fashioned harpoon and rawhide line.

Eskimo families are busy for days at a time making nets for

A simple Eskimo meal

catching fish and birds; extra-strong nets of sinew for catching seals; rawhide lines; spears; harpoons; and fishing gear. These as well as steel traps and guns are the tools the hunter uses to secure food from the sea and the tundra.

Many Eskimos are crack shots with rifles. The best marksmen are chosen to do the shooting for the boat crews hunting white whale, oogruk, and walrus. Girls as well as boys learn to shoot when quite young. The rabbits and ptarmigan for many meals are shot or trapped by schoolboys and schoolgirls.

When hunting and fishing are good, there is plenty to eat for everyone and food is stored for the "hungry time" that may come.

Storms and ice and dangerous tides may keep the hunters at home and food supplies become dangerously low. Even today periods of starvation occur in some of the villages; but severe famines are rare, because more care is used in gathering and storing food than formerly, and there is more cash income for buying store foods.

The hair seal—the same rascal that tears the fishermen's nets in southeast Alaska—and his much larger relative, the oogruk, are sometimes referred to as the Eskimo staff of life. Without these animals for food and clothing the Eskimos would find it difficult to survive. If unfavorable weather conditions prevent the hunters from getting seals for several days, everybody worries, and there is great rejoicing when the first seal is brought into the village.

The women usually do the work of skinning and preparing the seal and oogruk that are shot and dragged home by the men. They carefully skin the carcasses and save the hides for boat coverings, boot soles, and many other useful articles. Thick chunks of blubber are cut away from the meat and dropped into a sealskin bag, sometimes called a "seal poke." The poke is tied up and stored in a cool place. The thin clear seal oil separates or renders from the blubber and is drawn off as needed. Fresh seal oil is nearly odorless and has a bland flavor. Nothing tastes better to an Eskimo boy or girl than strips of dried salmon or reindeer meat dipped in seal oil. The rancid or inferior oil is burned in seal-oil lamps, or is sometimes mixed with corn meal, rice screenings, or other cheap cereals imported for dog food. After the fat is taken off, the seal carcasses are split and hung to dry. The dried seal meat is then used during the winter as food for both people and dogs. Of course a great deal of it is eaten fresh; seal or oogruk liver is considered a delicacy by the Eskimos.

The walrus is almost as important a food animal as is the seal. However, walrus herds are scarce, so they cannot be depended on for a regular supply. An average-sized walrus will supply several hundred pounds of meat, a large quantity of blubber, skin covering for oomiaks, and often a quantity of ivory from the tusks. Until

A beluga whale

a few years ago the walrus herds were often hunted for their ivory alone, and tons of meat were wasted. But now laws have been passed which protect the herds by prohibiting the killing of walrus for any purpose except obtaining food. White men are allowed to hunt and kill walrus only by special permission from the Alaska Game Commission.

As soon as the sea ice begins to break up in the spring, from April to June, the whales migrate to the Arctic. The easiest whale to catch, and the most common, is the small white whale called the beluga; however, a beluga may weigh as much as a thousand pounds.

The most exciting and dangerous hunt is for the large bowhead whale. All oomiaks, paddles, lines, harpoons, floats, guns, and other equipment must be in the best condition when the hunters start out to make their whaling camp at the edge of the ice pack. The men must watch every minute for changes in wind and shore current and for the dreaded breaks in the pack which can suddenly endanger their lives. Sometimes great blocks of ice break off and swiftly spin away in the strong current, carrying the hunters out to sea. Dramatic rescues have been made by boat, and even by small airplanes and helicopters, but many a brave hunter has been lost forever.

When the big bowheads have been shot, harpooned, and pulled alongside the ice pack they are quickly butchered, so the meat can be brought into the village by dog team—or by boat, if the ice has receded from the shore. Hundreds of pounds of blubber and meat are put away in the ice caves, and everyone is happy, because the village now has a good supply of food. At the end of a successful whaling season a great celebration is held, known all along the Arctic shores as the "Nelukataktut."

Just as Eskimos could not live without the seals, walrus, and other animals and birds taken from the sea and land, neither could they live without many kinds of fish taken from the sea, rivers, and swamps of their Arctic homeland. During the summer fishing season, nets are hung at low tide on a line of stakes that extend out from the shore. When the tide rises, the salmon following the shoreline are caught in the nets. At the next low tide the captured fish are collected and the nets are set again. This kind of net is called a "gill net." It is designed to catch the fish by the gills as they try to swim through the meshes.

Salmon is one of nature's gifts to the people of the north. Unlike the fishermen of southeast Alaska, the Eskimos catch most of their salmon for use at home rather than for sale to canneries. Every family has plenty of fresh salmon to eat during the fishing season. But hundreds of fish must be dried for the winter months. These fish are split from head almost to tail, on each side of the backbone. Then the bones and entrails are cut out, leaving the thick meaty halves connected at the tail, and deep crosswise slashes are made,

A "gill net" at low tide

so the meat will dry more evenly. Next, the halves are dipped in brine and hung on crude wooden racks to dry in the sun and wind. Smudge fires are built under the fish to hasten the drying, keep away flies, and add a delicious smoky flavor to the meat. Choice fish are cut into long strips to be dried and smoked. These are so good that they are often called "Alaska candy." The Eskimos hope for dry and sunny weather; if the fish hang in fog and rain for a long time they lose their fine flavor and many of them spoil.

In certain places along the sea coast there is a summer run of herring, which are caught—a large school of them at a time—in small nets. Tough grass stems are threaded through the gills of these small fish and then braided into long strings. Then the herring are hung to dry and stored for winter use.

Besides the summer fishing, gardening is a profitable summer activity for many thrifty families. However, the Eskimo gardener,

Fish cut into strips

like the coastal-village gardener, must be content with only the crops that grow quickly in the cool topsoil of the Arctic, such as cabbages, turnips, carrots, and potatoes. Although the growing season is short, the vegetables grow twenty-four hours a day during the continuous sunlight of summer. The village of Unalakleet is famous for its gardens. Fresh vegetables from these gardens are sometimes shipped by airplane to Nome, where they are sold for good prices. Many villages along the Kobuk and Noatak Rivers have their vegetable gardens. Gardeners must buy their seeds a year ahead, for planting time comes long before the sea ice leaves the shore and the supply ship brings its annual cargo.

Emptying a fish trap

During the spring and summer months the women and older children gather willow buds for greens; also cranberries and blueberries. These are eaten fresh, put away in seal oil, or frozen for winter use. This is also the season when wild geese, ducks, cranes, puffins, and sea parrots are shot or caught in nets. Many of these are stored in ice caves for winter use. Small boys are lowered over the cliffs on sealskin ropes to gather birds' eggs from the nests in the rocks. This is exciting and dangerous—but the eggs will taste good the following winter, when a little variety in diet will be greatly appreciated!

Indeed, during the winter months fresh foods are limited to a few kinds of fish, and these are very hard to get. Along the Yukon and Kuskokwim Rivers and other large streams one may catch such winter fish as whitefish, ling, and chee fish in large traps set under the ice. The traps are like large basketwork funnels. Some are made of wire netting over a framework of poles. When the ice is several feet deep, a group of men will work a day or more to dig a large rectangular hole through it, and anchor the trap in the running water below. The trap must be raised and emptied once or twice a week—a very hard job if the ice freezes to a greater depth between visits. If the fish have been running well, there will be some for several families and even something for the dogs. Live fish from the traps freeze quickly in the cold air when they are dipped out of the trap. But they must be tossed well back from the hole, so they won't flop back into the water!

Inland on the tundra small blackfish and still smaller needlefish are found at the bottom of streams, where the water remains unfrozen under many feet of ice and snow. These fish are caught in small basket-like traps made of wooden strips bound together with willow twigs. Digging a hole through the ice to set one of these traps is a long, cold job.

During the winter Eskimos who live near the ocean "jig" for a small mackerel-like fish called a tomcod. For this kind of fishing a hole is dug, not too far from shore, through the ice under which the tomcod live for the winter months. Through this hole, the Eskimo fisherman (or woman) lowers a line of finely split whalebone carrying a barbless hook. The whalebone is better than cotton or linen because the water will not freeze on it. The line is alternately raised and lowered, and this is called "jigging." The hook is not baited, but depends for its effectiveness on snagging the fish as they swim by. Two sticks are required to keep the line moving and to knock the fish off without getting mittens wet. When the fisherman feels a tug, he jerks the line upward, firmly attached to the first stick, and uses his second stick to raise it further, but carrying part of the line horizontally. By a quick

An Eskimo woman "jigging" for fish

move with the first stick, he catches another section of the line, and raises this. Thus, moving his two sticks back and forth as long as need be, he "weaves" the line until the fish is out of water, and shaken onto the ice, far enough from the hole so that he cannot flip back. Actually, the line is relatively short, so landing the fish is a matter of seconds. When fishing is good, fifty or sixty pounds of these fish may be caught in a single afternoon. Often the Eskimo women and children go jigging for tomcod while the men are doing harder work, such as hunting, lifting fish traps, or hauling wood. Pike are caught through the ice of inland rivers and ponds in much the same way as the tomcod. Sometimes the fish are cooked, but more often the frozen fish are cut into bite-sized chunks and eaten raw.

Eskimos are very fond of a special delicacy called "Eskimo ice-cream" by white people. Melted reindeer fat or seal oil is beaten with fresh clean snow until it forms a creamy mass. Blueberries or bits of frozen meat may be folded into this rich "cream." The concoction is an ideal treat in this cold country, where plenty of fats must be eaten to help keep the body warm.

Nobody knows for how many hundreds of years Eskimos have made clothing and footwear from the hides of seals and caribou and from the soft warm pelts of fox, beaver, wolf, squirrel, wolverine, and other animals. From the time she is a little girl learning to make doll clothes, until she becomes a grandmother, the Eskimo woman is tanner, tailor, bootmaker, and seamstress. Not only does she make her own patterns, but she is an expert in many kinds of needlecraft. Besides the special techniques of fur-sewing, she learns to knit, darn, embroider, and to make most of the cloth clothing her family needs. Her best friends are her hand-powered sewing machine and her ivory needle case.

These skillful tailors of the north are wise in the lore of skinning and tanning. They know which pelts are warmest, which are waterproof. They know how to fashion the skin from the legs of a caribou into the tops of a pair of man's boots. They can easily shape the skin from the head of a caribou fawn into a parka hood for a boy or girl. The Eskimo parka is so well designed as a cold-weather garment that the pattern has been borrowed for the clothing of soldiers who must live and fight in cold countries. How to keep warmly dressed in frigid temperatures is one of the important lessons the Eskimos have taught us.

A man's parka is usually made of reindeer or caribou skin with a wolfskin ruff to protect the face from the bitter north winds. In the coldest weather a hunter will wear two parkas, the inner one without a ruff and with the fur turned inside. If he can afford woolen underwear, woolen trousers, and a shirt, he wears these

A man's parka

under his parka. His fur boots are made of skin from reindeer legs. His boot soles are of the heavy waterproof hide of a large seal called a "mukluk" by the Eskimos; for this reason the boots themselves are called "mukluks." Cotton work gloves, worn under fur mittens, protect his hands. Sometimes he wears a denim work parka and dungarees over his fur clothing, especially if he is doing dirty work, such as butchering.

For dress wear, women and older girls have spotted reindeer or squirrel-skin parkas. The large light-colored ruff around the face is of wolf, especially chosen for its long silvery guard hairs which stand out, making a soft oval frame several inches in width. The

Calico-covered reindeer and spotted squirrel-skin parkas

dark fur used to make a sort of inner frame next to the face and throat is of wolverine. Frost from the breath does not collect as readily on wolverine as it does on other fur, so the wearer's face will be warm and dry in the coldest weather. Tiny strips of this fur are also used for decorative trimming at the shoulders, both in front and back. V-shaped strips of white deerskin, embroidered or beaded, may be inserted at the shoulders. Small pieces of light and dark deerskin, sewn into a geometric pattern, often form a band around the bottom of the garment just above a narrow fringe of

Girl's parka trimmed with beads and bells

wolfskin. Mittens of white dogskin and white reindeer boots often complete the costume.

Little girls' parkas must be beautiful too. Only the softest, light gray wolfskin with the darkest wolverine next to the face make up the ruff. Decorative inserts for the shoulders and the border trim, and sometimes a bit of glitter from beads or trinkets, make the fashionable garment dear to the heart of every little girl.

A mother must know how to make skin clothing for tiny babies. She must also know just how much extra room to allow in the hood

Baby travels in hood of mother's parka

of her own parka so that her baby will have plenty of squirming space and a snug, warm place to ride!

When the white traders brought cloth to Alaska the native people quickly found many uses for it. Women and children have homemade parka covers of bright cotton prints, bordered with wide ruffles. These are worn over the fur parkas in the colder

Twisting fibers into sinew thread

weather. In warm weather the parka cover may be worn without the fur garment underneath. Washable parka covers for the men and boys are made of heavy denim or canvas.

Parka covers not only protect the fur parkas from wear and soil; they also keep them from getting wet in stormy weather. Covers are worn in sleet storms, snowstorms, or blizzards, as the snow does not stick to the cotton as it does to fur. White cotton parkas help a man to hide against the snow when he is creeping up to shoot seals and other game.

The Eskimo woman is expert at skinning the animals her husband kills, and at tanning the hides or pelts and making them into clothing. She also makes her own sinew thread, which is much better than cotton or linen thread for sewing fur clothing. The strong bands of sinew are pulled from the backs and legs of reindeer and caribou when they are butchered. This sinew is carefully

Scraped seal hides stretched on poles for bleaching

dried and shredded into fine fibers. Then, with the help of fingers and lips, the fibers are twisted into a firm, even thread.

Preparing the skins for clothing and footwear is hard, tedious work. In summer, seal hides are pegged down on the tundra to dry

Crimping leather to form a boot sole

and bleach in the wind and sun. Many hours must be spent scraping flesh and fat from a bearskin before it can be tanned.

In winter, scraped seal hides are stretched on poles to freeze and bleach. The finished leather, called "luftak," is used for the soles of fur boots. It is tough and nearly waterproof. The women know the secret of making waterproof seams where the boot soles are sewn to the boot tops. Sometimes strips of luftak are dyed, usually red, for welting and for ties.

With her strong teeth the Eskimo woman crimps tiny tucks into the margins of a piece of luftak to form a boot sole that will fit properly around the heels and toes, according to the size of the wearer. Neighbors can recognize one another's work by the marks of the teeth on the leather. Sometimes a woman uses a blunt knife to crimp the leather.

Nothing is more important than good boots with warm insoles if one is out very long in sub-zero temperatures. Cotton or wool felt insoles may be bought from the trader, but these must be changed and dried out often. If they get damp from perspiration or snow, or packed down firmly, they won't hold warmth. Instead of manufactured insoles in their boots many prefer shaped wads of dry tundra grass, because these can be easily fluffed and dried. Besides, tundra grass is free for the gathering. On a long, cold trip it is important to wear strong trail boots, roomy enough to go over warm fawnskin foot socks made with the fur inside.

Food, clothing, housing, fuel—clever as he is at taking most of these necessities from the land and sea, the Eskimo must have some money. Every family has to be able to buy some food and manufactured articles shipped from the States on the annual supply steamer. Flour, sugar, evaporated milk, coffee, tea, rice, soap, and canned and dried fruits are used by most families. Hunters need rifle and shotgun shells, guns and traps, outboard motors, gasoline, matches, tents, and many kinds of tools and hardware. The women need calico, denim, beads, scissors, needles, yarn, and pots and pans. Dishes, beds, stoves, linoleum, sewing machines, even radios and musical instruments, are found in many homes. Frequently the trader's stock includes lollipops and candy bars, pocket knives, hair ribbons, and a few toys.

How does the Eskimo get the money he needs to buy these things? Both the men and women work for wages whenever they get the opportunity; they are considered good workers. A few work in the salmon canneries in the Bristol Bay area every summer. The companies send airplanes to bring them to the canneries and to return them to their summer homes after the canning season. Others work as janitors, firemen, and maintenance men in the village schools and hospitals. They drive tractors and trucks. Some are employed to help service planes. A few are airplane pilots.

Many work in mines and on big gold dredges that operate during the summer months, digging gold from the ancient stream beds. Others work as longshoremen, and as engineers and deckhands on the river boats and small ships that run along the coast during the summer. The women often serve as cooks in hospitals and mine camps. A few are employed in private homes as housekeepers and nursemaids, or in hospitals as attendants. Those who are professionally trained work as teachers and nurses.

Some of the men are expert ivory-carvers. They make beautiful bracelets, necklaces, paperweights, and pen stands representing Arctic birds and animals, as well as figurines, bookmarks, and many other articles to be sold to tourists. With a good supply of ivory, and plenty of time, an industrious craftsman may add a hundred dollars or so to his yearly income in this way. Skilled ivory-carvers are sometimes employed as instructors to teach this craft to schoolboys. Other saleable articles include fine dolls for which collectors often pay well. These dolls, with heads carved from ivory or wood, are carefully dressed in fur clothing—each garment an exact miniature of one worn by Eskimo people. Baskets of grass and whalebone, fur slippers, and other Eskimo-made items can be turned in to the trading post for the tourist trade.

In the winter the men often trap furs. Fox furs—red, white, and silver—are brought in by the trappers and traded for many necessities. These furs, as well as mink, beaver, muskrat, marten, and other kinds are sent to fur markets in the States. They are one of the most important sources of income for many families. Store managers and traders become experts at judging the quality and market value of many kinds of furs.

In Nome a group of Eskimos has organized a company for making and selling Eskimo fur garments and footwear. The company buys parkas, mittens, and mukluks made by women in villages many miles away. There is a good market for genuine Eskimo fur garments both in Alaska and in certain parts of the States. Admiral Richard E. Byrd and his men went to the South Pole dressed in clothing made by these Arctic seamstresses. (There were several Eskimo men in his crew, and many of the sled dogs used by the Byrd expedition were bought from natives who had raised them as pups and trained them on Alaska trails.)

Busy as they are with all the problems of getting food and clothing, and making a living, Eskimo parents stay in their home villages as much as possible, to enable their children to attend school. All but the smallest villages have schools. In the schoolhouse are one or two classrooms, the teacher's quarters, a shop, an office and a small clinic. The building also serves as a meeting place for the village council, for parties and dances, and for other important gatherings. Trained Eskimo teachers are employed whenever possible. Their mastery of both the English and Eskimo languages and their understanding of the ways of their own people aid them in becoming successful teachers.

As in schools everywhere, arithmetic, history, and geography must be studied. The white man's language, his books, pencils, paper, pictures, and maps soon become familiar to Eskimo boys and girls. Music is a favorite subject—singing time is always a happy time at school. Good health habits are taught and practiced, so that children learn how to have clean bodies and clean clothes in spite of little water and scarce fuel.

Men and boys enjoy working in the school shop. Sometimes a skilled older craftsman is engaged to carry out a special teaching project with a group of boys, such as making a kayak, snowshoes, or a sled. Every boy is expected to know how to construct and repair many kinds of equipment that he will use as a hunter, fisherman, and trapper.

In the more isolated Arctic the school radiophone is the only way of exchanging messages and news with the rest of the world for weeks at a time during the short stormy days of winter when the mail planes are often unable to fly. At a certain time in the evening the teacher may call the nearest doctor by radiophone, to tell him about the sick people in the village, and to get his

Boy, supervised by a skilled craftsman, building a kayak

suggestions for the treatment and care of the patients. As in the coastal villages, when someone is seriously ill or injured the doctor may send a small airplane to bring the patient to one of the hospitals in the area. When bad weather holds up the plane for many days, family and friends spend anxious days and nights praying for good weather and listening for the plane.

A traveling public-health nurse is an occasional visitor. One of her big jobs is to teach the people how to care for their children, especially the babies; how to have cleaner homes; how to keep food clean and pure and to improve diets, using native foods; how to give sick people the proper attention and to protect members

Father Tom Cunningham, S.J.

of the family from contagious diseases. Since there is seldom a doctor to help when babies are born, the nurses also teach certain women in the village to be midwives.

Missionaries also are occasional visitors. Many well-known denominations have churches and missions in the Arctic as well as in other parts of Alaska. The Presbyterian Mission Church at Point Barrow is one of the largest churches in the Eskimo territory. In this farthest-north Presbyterian outpost there is a comfortable home provided for the resident missionary and his family.

The Roman Catholic Church has priests and missions in many Arctic villages. Famous among them is Father Tom Cunningham, S.J., who was for many years priest on Little Diomede Island.

Tools and guns placed on poles near a grave

"Father Tom," as he is called, is one of the few white men who have learned to speak Eskimo.

The Episcopal Church has established headquarters for its traveling missionary at Point Hope. In the Episcopal Mission cemetery in this village huge whalebones serve as grave-markers. A fence of whale ribs keeps prowling foxes and wolves away from the graves.

Farther south, there is the Russian Church at St. Michael, which has become a famous landmark in the Arctic. The Methodists have established a church at Nome. A Swedish Evangelical church has long been established at Unalakleet, and several groups of Seventh

Seesaw, Eskimo style

Day Adventists are scattered from Seward Peninsula to the Bristol Bay area. Bethel is headquarters for the active Moravian group that has established several missions in the tundra lands of the Kuskokwim.

Although Christian organizations have been active in the Arctic for many years, a few ancient religious beliefs and customs still prevail in some of the more isolated small villages. In places where it is too swampy or too frozen to dig graves, the dead are placed in boxes on top of the ground. Guns, tools, sewing machines, and many things that were used by the dead while they were alive are placed on poles near the burial boxes, in the belief that these articles will be needed by the spirits of the departed persons.

In addition to school and church activities, Eskimos devote time from their work to recreation. They are naturally a gay and laughing people, and they enjoy getting together just to enjoy them-

Eskimo child with dog

selves. Almost every village has a "kashim," or native community house; this is actually an oversize igloo where the people gather to take part in old-time dances. The drummers make a perfect rhythm with their big flat drums, and sing songs that tell stories of long ago or about hunting adventures. Both the men and women dance to these songs, dramatizing the action of the stories.

Polar-bear cub

A popular out-of-door game is a special Eskimo style of "see-saw." Partners stand on opposite ends of a plank, balanced over a log that lies on the ground. When each player jumps on his end of the plank, his partner is tossed high in the air. A skillful player will keep his balance and land on his end of the plank after each toss. Some Eskimo boys and girls learn to jump many times without missing.

In every village there are always the friendly pups of the mon-

Playing in the frame of an old oomiak

grel sled dogs that are ready for a frisky adventure with anyone, young or old. No child can resist a rough-and-tumble game with such a frolicsome pet.

Occasionally a hunter brings into the village a polar-bear cub whose mother has been killed. Though still young, the cub is very savage and dangerous and must be kept chained. When he grows a little larger he may be killed for his hide. However, it is sometimes possible to sell an animal like this to a zoo in the States. If he is sold he will be put into a very strong crate and taken by airplane to Fairbanks, to start the long journey by rail and steamer to his new home.

During the long days of summer Eskimo children are free

to roam the beaches and nearby tundra, to play tag and jump rope. They frequently play imaginative games, such as killing wolves, wrestling with bears, or hunting walrus in the frame of an old oomiak. In the farthest-north villages there is no regular summer bedtime hour for anyone. When the children can stay awake no longer, they simply curl up in their summer parkas and go to sleep wherever they are.

It is pleasant for older people to rest and visit out-of-doors on these fine, warm days. Everyone knows that the long cold winter will soon return, when there will be no sunlight for many weeks. Then the fifty-below-zero weather and howling storms will keep everybody indoors for days at a time. But while the summer's long hours of daylight last, everyone makes the most of out-of-door living. The Eskimo has learned to be content with what each day brings.

CHAPTER VI

Arctic Reindeer Round-up

Fifty years ago the Eskimos of Alaska often suffered from food shortages. White whalers were killing off the whales and walrus. At times seals and fish, birds and rabbits, were scarce. For some unknown reason, the great herds of caribou drifted to the east, away from the coast, and at that time could not be found by hunters. Starvation was common.

It was necessary for the government to do something to help these people build up the food supply in the Arctic. After a great deal of study it seemed wise to try to establish reindeer herds in Alaska. Observers reported that there was plenty of "reindeer moss," a special kind of white lichen necessary as food for the deer, on the Arctic slopes and tundra lands. About twelve hundred deer were brought over from Siberia and distributed in little herds throughout the Eskimo country. Lapp herders were brought along to teach the Eskimos how to care for the animals and how to use the methods of "close herding" as practiced in Lapland. This involved keeping the deer in herds, and moving them deliberately from grazing area to grazing area, in such a manner as to prevent over-grazing. This also meant that there were always men and dogs with the herd, which tended to control wolves. It also kept

Summer round-up of reindeer herd

the deer tame. Conditions were so favorable that the deer increased and everything went well for a few years, until there were sizable herds of deer in several areas, from Bristol Bay to Point Barrow.

Then several things happened to jeopardize this new source of food and clothing for the Eskimo. Gradually many of the herds fell into the hands of white owners, who sent thousands of pounds of meat as well as the hides to markets in the States. These white owners used the "open herding" techniques of the western cattle ranges. Herders were employed only to round up the deer for branding and killing. The deer became wild, and tended to overgraze certain areas. They also tended to disperse, and there was evidence that they were likely to adopt the caribou "cycle," drifting eastward out of the Eskimo coastal area at times. This loosening of the herds brought wolves into the region, and at the time the white owners were bought out, hundreds of deer a year were being slaughtered by the wolves. The wolves often ate only the tongues and livers of the killed deer—sometimes not even these, so that it looked as though some wolves killed for the fun of it.

When the market price of deer meat dropped, the remaining deer, no longer profitable, were allowed to range over the tundra without care. Where the animals were plentiful many of them were killed for dog food, and much meat was wasted. Wolf packs increased rapidly. Wolves were probably more responsible than anything else for the destruction of the herds over wide areas.

Conditions became so bad that the government came to the rescue and in 1937 bought all the remaining white-owned deer that could be found on the range. Today the reindeer are managed under government supervision for the benefit of the natives. White men are no longer allowed to own deer. Better methods of herding, marking, and ownership accounting have been developed. Also, efforts are being made to exterminate the wolves. The Eskimos depend on the deer not only for part of their food and clothing but also for a limited amount of cash, since some of the meat and the Arctic clothing made from the hides may be sold. Most white people in the north buy reindeer meat, deerskin parkas, and boots from the Eskimos.

The reindeer graze on the tundra and low hills of Alaska much as do cattle on the range in the American West. But there are no cowboys on horses in Alaska to care for the herds. Horses could not endure the cold Arctic winters; neither could they find the right kind of grass or hay or grain in the reindeer country. So the reindeer herders must travel on foot during the summertime; in the winter they use snowshoes or travel with dog teams. The herder knows that he must stay close to the deer to protect them from the wolves, being well aware that a pack of hungry wolves can kill several deer and scatter a big herd in just a few minutes.

Twice a year round-ups are held on the reindeer range. July and August are the months for the big round-ups for butchering. Smaller round-ups are held in February. Before the round-ups, airplanes are sent out to "spot" the scattered bands of deer and to leave additional herders with them. The deer must be driven many miles into the corrals near the coast. Here some of the steers, some of the bulls, and the old cows are butchered, leaving only healthy young stock to increase the herd. A few fawns are killed for their skins, which are then used for parkas, warm fur socks, and other kinds of clothing.

The meat is put into cold-storage until a ship comes for it. Usually the same ship that brings the year's supply of store goods to the village takes the meat away. The meat is sold in many Alaska towns and in a few places in the States. Some of the hides are shipped to glove factories and to other manufacturers of leather goods.

At the round-up in February only enough animals are butchered for local use. The chief herder decides at which corral the round-up will be held and sends word to other villages. For weeks before the round-up, herders drive small bands of deer toward the corral. The bands combine into one large herd of several thousand deer, closely guarded by the herders on the range a few miles from the corral. Wolves sometimes stampede the animals, and days of work are needed to get the deer back together again. It is important to limit the herd and keep it moving so the deer may find enough reindeer moss. At this time of year it is often difficult for the deer to dig down far enough through the deep snow to reach the moss.

While the herders are driving the reindeer in for the round-up other workers are putting up a camp of tents near the corral. Whole families come to the round-up, for there will be much fun and visiting as well as hard work. The women take turns in the "grub tent," where meals are cooked for the herders. Gallons of thick reindeer stew, huge reindeer roasts and chops and steaks,

Winter round-up camp

hundreds of hot-cakes and biscuits, and countless pots of coffee will be consumed. The camp is noisy and exciting. Almost every family comes in a sled drawn by seven or nine dogs. Every time a new team arrives, or if anything unusual happens, all the dogs bark and howl in a chorus. There may be several hundred dogs in the camp by the time everybody has arrived.

For several days before the round-up begins, the men and boys are busy repairing the corral. Holes in the log-and-brushwood fence must be mended, or filled in with big blocks of snow, to keep the deer from escaping. The corral is shaped like a huge funnel. The large open end is made of fences called "wings." These fences are often over a mile long, and they may be more than a mile apart

Model reindeer corral

at the open end of the funnel. The spout of the funnel narrows into a string of three pens or corrals; the second is smaller than the first, and the third—the working pen—is the smallest of all. The tip of the funnel is a narrow chute leading from the third pen; through this handling chute the deer are driven to be counted or branded.

Waiting for the round-up to begin is as exciting as waiting for a circus. Finally a herder dashes into camp behind a fast team of

Coffee break

dogs. He says there are over a thousand deer gathered on the range a few miles from the corral. The boss herder decides that the round-up will start early the next morning. Everyone crawls into his sleeping bag early, thinking of the big day to come.

By seven o'clock the men and boys are on their way out to surround a band of about four hundred deer that the herders have separated from the main herd and have driven up near the wings of the corral. Everyone is on snowshoes. There is no shouting or racing—the boss herder has told everybody to be as quiet as possible, to keep from exciting the deer. For the same reason all sled dogs are left at camp. Several boys are sent to the corral to make sure that no stray dogs get close enough to frighten the deer as they come into the wings of the corral. A few collie dogs, especially trained to work with reindeer, are taken along with the herders. These dogs know how to head off the stray deer and keep them traveling with the herd.

Within an hour or two the small band of deer are safely inside the wings of the corral and are being driven slowly toward the "holding corral," the first large pen. By now the sun is above the horizon, and the glare from the snow is blinding. The temperature, which has been nearly thirty-five degrees below zero during the night, begins to rise slowly. It may go as high as twenty degrees below zero during the middle of the day!

Hard work and cold air make midmorning and midafternoon coffee most welcome! Often there are doughnuts or hot biscuits to go with it. The girls have a grand time arguing about who will carry the heavy coffeepot and food boxes from the grub tent to the corral, where they stay as long as possible to watch the fun.

Inside the holding corral the deer mass themselves into a closely packed circle. They walk or trot around this circle, always moving or "milling" in a clockwise direction. When tired they may stop milling and lie down or stand quietly. Unlike cattle or sheep, these animals do not bellow or bleat. Reindeer make no noise other than a low grunt, which they repeat monotonously when excited. Anyone expecting to see a handsome, sleek, alert animal like the glamorous, lacy-antlered creatures driven by Santa Claus will be deeply disappointed! Alaskan reindeer are rough and shaggy, slow to learn, and usually very timid—though once in a while an old male will lower his horns and threaten to charge a man or dog. They generally try very hard to run away and will make desperate attempts to jump over the corral fence. Moving slowly and quietly, a person may get quite close to a herd. But a sudden movement or

Boys, girls, and burlap form a moving fence

shout will send the whole herd galloping to the far side of the corral or out to the open range, if the deer find a way to escape.

When the herders are ready to start branding, small bunches of twenty to thirty deer are separated from the band in the holding corral. To do this, the boys and girls, together with some of the men and women who have come just to enjoy the excitement, form into a line, carrying a long strip of burlap. With this moving fence, the end boy farthest from the gate to which the deer will be driven works his way into the herd and "cuts out" twenty or more deer. The other members of the living fence follow; soon this little band of deer is separated from the larger group and is guided into the next pen, called the "working pocket."

The timid animals do not try to break through the moving fence, although a badly frightened one will sometimes jump over a sagging stretch. With a clatter of horns and hoofs and a chorus of grunts they gallop in a circle partly surrounded by the burlap

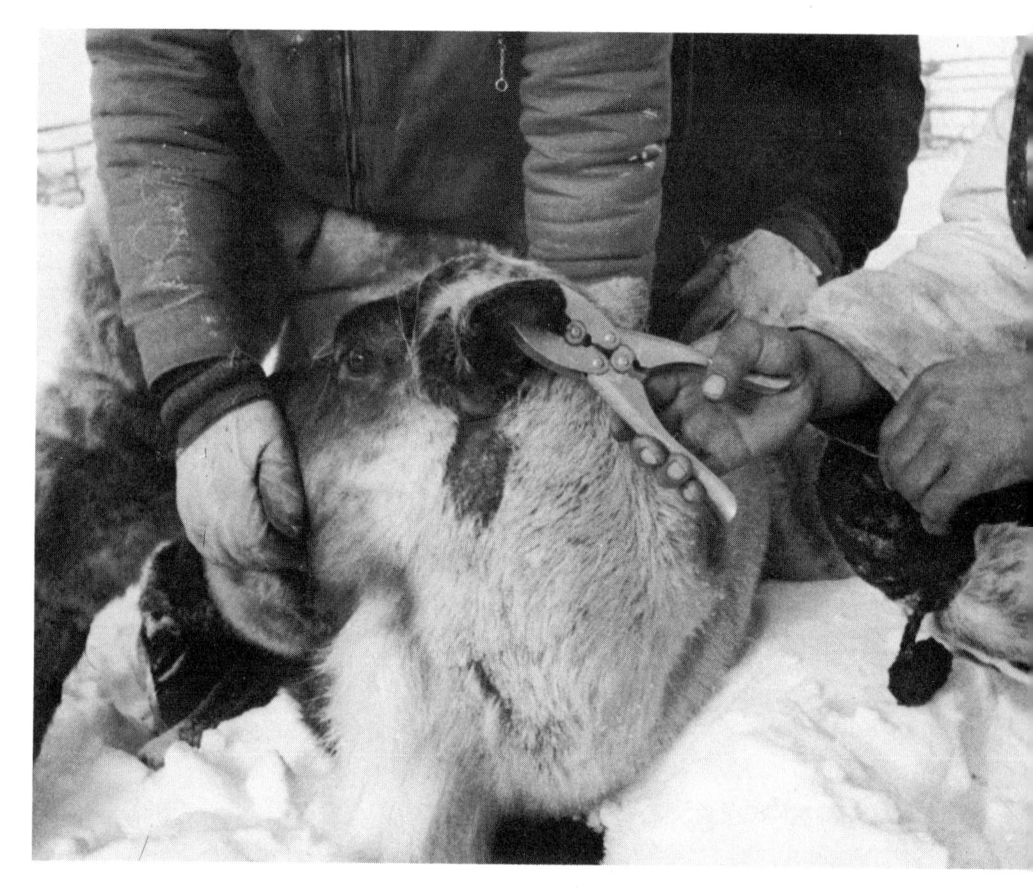

Branding a deer with an aluminum tag

fence. The steam from their breath hangs in the cold air, partly hiding them from view. Running ahead of the moving fence, the deer finally enter the working pocket and the gate is closed behind them. From this small pen they are driven one by one through the chute. Dividing small bands of deer from the large herd in this way is called "blanketing off," because of the old custom of using blankets stretched between the people who were the walking fenceposts. Bolts of burlap—hundreds and hundreds of yards—make the much better moving fences used today, but the old name for the procedure is still used.

Reindeer have such heavy coats of coarse hair that they cannot be easily branded with hot irons, as cattle and horses are branded in the States, so they are branded by cutting notches in the edges of their ears or by punching a numbered aluminum tag into their ears with a tool that looks very much like a pair of pliers. Every owner has a mark of his own, or a number. At the round-ups each deer is carefully counted and two men are given the job of recording the markings as they are called out from the handling chute.

Sometimes a frightened reindeer will run or jump wildly when it is caught for examination or marking. Then a strong man will seize the deer by the horns and with a mighty twist throw the animal to the ground for the necessary work. This way of handling a deer is called "bulldogging," a term borrowed from the cowboys in the States who handle cattle in this way. Many deer can be identified or marked in the handling chute without being thrown; however, for much of the work of the round-up the animals must be bulldogged.

The spring round-ups usually take from three days to a week. There is a great deal of work to do besides marking and butchering the deer. Meat must be frozen and packed for the return trip by dog team to the home villages. Hides must be scraped and rolled up. A round-up is exciting and very hard work. But after the first day or two much of the excitement dies down; everybody gets very tired and is rather glad when the work is over. Tents are taken down; kettles, leftover food, and sleeping bags are packed into the sleds. The yelping dogs, eager to leave, jerk and leap in their harnesses. There are many dog fights before the teams are finally on the trail and everyone is happily homeward bound. Happiest of all are the deer—in the distance seen heading rapidly toward the open range.

CHAPTER VII

Life in an Interior Indian Village

To the Indians of Interior Alaska home is the valley of the Yukon River and its branches. Their little log cabins are scattered from the Canadian border in the east to the tundra in the west. They are at home on the Chandalar, the Black, and the Porcupine Rivers. They roam the hills of the Koyukuk to the north. They follow the valley of the Tanana River, and drift south along the Alaska Highway, where they seek work in the road camps and airfields. A few have left the valley of the Yukon and its side streams to wander into the valleys of the Copper and the upper Kuskokwim Rivers.

But wherever they are, the river is their friend. It is their summer highway, their winter trail, their year-round airstrip. The tiny freight boats that ply the rivers bring them supplies from the outside world.

The wooded areas along the rivers and streams provide logs for houses and fuel. Boys learn early to be expert axmen in this land where one of nature's best gifts is the spruce forest. Men must be competent carpenters to build good, snug cabins. Small windows, doors, hinges, stovepipes, nails, and a few tools are bought from the trader. Everything else must come from the woods and

An Indian village in the Arctic

swamps. It takes months to build even a small cabin. The logs are cut, dragged in from the forest, and allowed to dry or season for a year. Then they are peeled; the ends are notched to make them fit together; and the walls slowly rise. If the builder is fortunate he will be able to buy a little lumber from the trader for door and window frames, for the floor, and for a few simple shelves and cupboards. Otherwise the lumber for frames and cupboards is cut from logs, a board at a time, with a big two-man saw.

Once the logs are in place for the walls, and the ridge log is securely pegged to the gables, small straight saplings are laid to form the roof. For weeks men and boys have been gathering moss

Hoist to lift buckets of earth to roof

in the swamps and packing it home on their backs and on pack dogs. Now a thick layer of this moss is laid over the roof poles. Next, tons of earth are lifted to the roof in buckets and spread evenly over the moss to form a warm, dry roof. Now the family may move into the new home. Little matter if there is only the earth for a floor until next year. On the roof, weeds and wild flowers soon begin to grow—the more the better, for the roots help to hold the soil against the heavy rains of fall and spring. If the family has good luck trapping muskrats, there may be enough money to buy corrugated metal roofing to lay over the earth roof. Then they will have a dry cabin for many years.

Since the home cabin is small, an even smaller cabin—the "cache"—is built nearby for storage. The cache is always built on

A cache for storage

poles well above the ground. This protects the dried fish from dogs, wolves, and other animal prowlers. To keep bears, wolverines, rats, and other good climbers from robbing the cache, wide strips of tin cut from empty five-gallon oil cans are nailed around the posts.

The cache may become a temporary home during the annual spring floods. When the river ice breaks, huge ice jams form. The rain-swollen rivers rise behind the ice jams and flood miles of land and many homes. Then families climb into the caches, where they sometimes huddle for days surrounded by the flood waters. They can only hope that the great chunks of ice floating by will not knock down their temporary refuges or their cabins. When the water finally goes down, they move back to their soggy, mud-filled cabins to salvage what they can of what the flood has left, and to start again to make their dwellings homelike.

Unlike their distant Eskimo neighbors on the treeless tundra and Arctic coast, the river Indians have plenty of firewood. But so much has been cut and burned that there is little good wood left near many of the older villages, and people must go miles to find small logs, which they pull home on sleds drawn by hand or by dog teams. A few villages, usually where cooperative stores have grown up, have community-owned tractors that are used for hauling wood from the forest to the village.

Wood stoves, made of empty oil drums, are very popular because they will burn four-foot logs. These larger logs burn more slowly and heat more evenly than do small pieces of wood. Time and hard work are saved by not having to saw the four-foot lengths into shorter pieces. Of course, shorter lengths must be cut for the quick hot fires in the cookstoves. The cooking fires help to heat the cabins. Green wood is mixed with dry because it gives off more heat and burns more slowly. Cutting and hauling the logs from the forest to the village, sawing and chopping the firewood, are tasks that take many long cold hours.

It is almost as hard to get a drink of water in a very cold country as it is in a hot dry desert. The streams and lakes are covered with ice so thick that a man must dig for hours with a sharp steel bar to reach the water. Left unused, a water hole made in this way freezes over and must be dug out again. At forty below zero, ice and snow are much colder than ordinary refrigerator ice cubes. If a traveler should put some of the Arctic ice or snow in his mouth he would freeze his lips and tongue, resulting in painful frostbite that would blister and burn. To get a drink on the trail the traveler must find dry wood, build a fire, and melt ice or snow. Natives often carry Primus stoves as part of their trail equipment. Those who are fortunate enough to have Thermos bottles may take along a limited amount of hot water, tea, or coffee. A canteen of water hung at the belt—as in the desert—would not help; the water would soon be frozen solid.

As in the Eskimo country, the winter water supply for Interior

Carrying water with a neck yoke

Indian homes is carried from water holes to the barrels beside the cabin stoves. However, the Indian family can spare enough wood for a hand-carved neck yoke which enables one to carry two buckets of water at a time. When not in use the neck yoke hangs conveniently near the cabin door.

Also unlike the Eskimos, who seldom have year-round homes,

Ice blocks for the winter water supply

the Indians frequently store large amounts of ice for both winter and summer use in the Interior villages. Indian men and boys may bring several sledloads of the huge ice blocks at a time into the village—usually by dog team—and pile them high on special racks for winter use. In the summer the blocks are transferred to a summer storehouse and packed deep in sawdust.

In the small Alaskan villages a bath is usually an old-fashioned affair in a laundry tub on the floor in front of the cookstove. Often a sponge bath from a basin must do. In some villages the men enjoy steam baths. A small hut of earth-covered logs is the village bathhouse. An open fire built in the center to heat the hut also

Baby gets a daily bath

heats a bucket of water set on the stones that rim the fireplace. When the smoke has cleared and the hut is stifling hot, several men, wearing only breechcloths, crawl into the hut. One sprinkles water on the hot stones, and the men sweat freely in the hot steam.

A fish wheel

Some hold little bundles of wet grass or shavings in their mouths to make breathing easier. Instead of a washcloth, a handful of dry grass and tiny alder twigs is used for scrubbing. When a man has had all he can stand of the heat and steam and has rubbed himself clean he rushes out of the hut, grabs his clothes from the low roof where he left them while bathing, and, half-dressed, runs for home through the frosty air.

Laundry, too, is a problem during the long winter months. To have water means to have wood for fuel; either can be had in exchange only for hard work. The lively pink-cheeked children who come to school in fresh clean overalls or stiff starched dresses tell a story without words of mothers carrying wood and water and laboring over washboards and with old-fashioned flatirons.

Like their distant neighbors, the coastal Indians and the Eskimos, the river Indians depend on fish for much of their food. Best

Fish taken from the river quickly freeze

of all are the salmon. These fine fish fight their way upstream for hundreds of miles from the coast. The shallow, swirling currents of the Interior streams are much different from the deep open waters of the coast; it would be impossible for seine boats and trollers to operate in these waters. Here in the Interior, fish wheels are used to catch the river's best offering.

Slim spruce poles are fastened to a log axle to make the spokes of a wide water wheel. Paddles are built at the opposite ends of the two spokes. Baskets made of chicken wire are mounted at the ends of the two remaining spokes. Set on a raft, and anchored out

A cone-shaped fish trap

from the bank, the wheel turns slowly in the current. Salmon swimming upstream are scooped up in the baskets, from which they fall into the fish box as the wheel turns over. Frequent trips must be made to empty the fish box, especially in hot weather, when the salmon quickly spoil. Day and night the creaking, groaning axles make a sort of weird music for the village to hear.

But salmon are not the river's only gift of food. As in the Eskimo

Making a fish net

country whitefish, ling, and chee fish fresh from the ice-covered river are a welcome addition to the winter food supply. When plentiful, fresh fish may be shared even with the dogs. But to catch these fish from a river locked under three to five feet of solid ice is cold and hard work.

The Indian men make beautiful basket traps of willow twigs. A large hole is cut in the ice and the trap is anchored under it. After several days the ice is again cut from the hole, the trap is raised, and the fish are collected. In many places traps of wire netting stretched over wooden frames have taken the place of willow withes, bound together in the shape of a funnel.

Another way of catching fish in the winter is by stretching a net under the ice, across a part of the stream. These nets are made by the women from cotton string bought from the trader.

A moose

Indians, like the Eskimos, frequently catch pike on lines lowered through holes in the ice. When fishing is good, one fisherman may catch as much as fifty pounds of pike in a single day.

The forests and hills of the river valleys also yield a harvest of food for the Indians. Moose—among America's biggest game animals—are often shot for food. When a hunter brings in a moose, the whole village gathers for a feast. A special treat is moose-nose soup, made from the nose and large fleshy upper lip. Roasts, steaks, and stews of moose meat are favorites with everyone. Ground moose meat is jokingly called "mooseburger." The hide is carefully saved for moccasins. Many a cabin sports over its door the huge antlers of a moose killed by the hunter who lives there.

October is the time for hunting caribou and mountain sheep. Sometimes the caribou gather in large bands and migrate across the country to find new feeding grounds. The hunters watch the herds for days and when they see that the caribou will pass near a village, they plan to make their kill at a point from which it will be easy to carry the meat home. Caribou, like all other game animals, are protected by law. Each family is allowed only two animals a season. The carcasses are carried to the villages and stored on the cabin roofs or high in a cache, where the meat is safe from hungry dogs. Here it freezes, later to become steaks and stews during the cold winter days when there is little other game to be found.

The mountain sheep are the hardest to hunt of any of the animals in Alaska. Because they live in the high ranges far from the rivers they are difficult to find. It is a long, arduous task to carry the meat home, once the animal is shot, but it is a great delicacy, and everyone is delighted to have a small share.

In the lowlands along the Interior rivers wild geese and ducks are shot in the fall. Beaver and muskrats, which are hunted and trapped for their fur, are considered choice meat too. Muskrat meat is sometimes seen in fancy meat markets in the States labeled as "marsh hare." Black bears are found nearly everywhere and are often eaten.

The big Arctic hare, often called the "snowshoe rabbit," because of its large feet, is an important food animal. At times the abundance of these animals prevents severe hunger when other game animals are hard to find. Schoolboys and schoolgirls often set rabbit snares after school in the afternoon and visit them next day in hopes of having meat for supper. Special wire, something like

A porcupine

heavy picture wire, can be bought at the trading post for the snares. The boys and girls easily twist this wire into small nooses and hang them cleverly between the twigs in the low fencelike thickets through which the rabbits have to force their way on their winter hops. The trappers say, "A good rabbit year is a good fur year." Fox, lynx, and other furbearers depend on these big rabbits for food also.

Even the slow and prickly porcupine is sometimes used for food, but there is an unwritten law among the woodsmen of the north

A trapper returns hume

against needlessly killing one of these animals. Because he is slow and clumsy, "porky" is the only animal in the woods that a man can kill with a club if he is lost without food or gun. Singed clean of the long hair and needles, and roasted, the flesh of these big rodents is said to taste like pork.

The Indians, like the Eskimos, raise vegetables and pick berries during the summer months. They also buy many food items at the village stores and from mail-order companies with money earned working on the highways, on the dredges, or by trapping furs.

Indians love the rugged life of the trail and the trapline. Boys around ten or twelve often go with their fathers to the traplines and the trapping camps. Good trappers learn the habits of the beaver, mink, and wolverine, the fox and the lynx. They know how to bait and hide the traps, and how to make sure that the traps are free from human odor, which might warn the animals and leave the trapper with only an empty trap for all his work.

A trapline may be twenty miles or more in length. A man and his family may claim a certain small stream valley as their trapping ground. Others will not trap there without permission. The trapper usually travels with a small dog team. Small cabins or shelter camps are built about a day's journey apart. At the end of each wearisome day the trapper is grateful for these shelters, which save him the trouble of pitching a tent and making camp in the snow. The trapper's life is lonely, but he is very busy. He must get as much fur as possible during the short season allowed by law, so he stays close to his trapline. His visits home are all too short.

Many of the Indian women are skillful trappers. If they do not go to the distant traplines with their husbands they often have short traplines near the village, and sometimes they are happily surprised at the value of their catches. Hungry wolves or coyotes sometimes come close to a village. Since these animals are the enemies of many valuable furbearers, the Territory of Alaska pays a bounty of fifty dollars each for their pelts. The money from the bounty, as well as the warm mittens, caps, and parka ruffs that can be made from the skin makes a captured wolf or coyote a kind of furbearing "jackpot."

In the spring, whole families often leave the village to live in rough camps near the muskrat swamps. The weather is warmer now; the snow is thawing; and the days are longer. It is great fun to load the sleds with food, camping gear, and traps, even light boats which are needed to get back home again after the muskrat season, for then the ice is out of the river and the winter trail disappears. But at camp everyone works hard. Boys and girls, as well

A woman trapper with a coyote

as the men and women, are experts in trapping and shooting these big brown rats whose pelts bring many dollars to the family.

Indians are often more conservative and careful trappers than are white men. Near his trapline the Indian has his home, where he hopes to live many years. Well he knows the importance of leaving enough animals for breeding stock. The white trapper, on the other hand, often comes from a distant town or from the States. Usually his main interest lies in getting all the fur he can; he may never return to the area he has once trapped. He may even hire an airplane to take him to the wild lakes and remote valleys beyond the Indians' traplines, killing the furbearers in their wilderness homes where they rear their young. Indian leaders and game wardens are worried about the conservation of the fur animals and big game, especially in certain areas, where hard winters and greedy newcomers have killed off so much of the wild life.

But furs represent more than a limited cash income for the Interior Indians. For these people, as well as for the Eskimos, animal hides provide warm out-of-door clothing—parkas and boots. However, the Indians do not have reindeer; neither do they have seals and walrus as sources of waterproof leather. Caribou skins are commonly used for Indian parkas and boot tops. But boot soles are usually made from heavy mooseskin—a good material for this purpose during very cold weather, when the snow is dry. However, one must be careful when cutting holes through the ice for water or for fishing, because mooseskin is very porous, and it absorbs water like a blotter. Wet feet soon freeze at sub-zero temperatures. When the snow begins to melt, during the spring thaw, the Interior Indians buy rubber footwear—"shoepacs" or lumbermen's rubbers —which are usually available at trading posts. But throughout the dry winter months almost everybody in these villages wears mooseskin moccasins with felt insoles. For this reason the Interior Indians are often called the "moccasin people" of Alaska.

Mooseskins are difficult to tan, but Indian women are expert tanners, their techniques being similar to those used by Eskimo women. A heavy "green" moose hide just brought in by the hunter often weighs a hundred pounds or more. After the well-soaked skin is scraped free from hair, it is hung for weeks in the cold dry

Woman scraping a skin

air to bleach and dry. Then it is scraped again for many hours with a dull knife to make it soft and pliable.

Finally it is stretched on a crude frame of willow branches and

A moose hide stretched on a frame for smoking

smoked over a slow-burning alderwood fire. This gives it the characteristic golden-brown color and a pleasant pungent odor. Now the hide is ready for use. The moccasins are cut by pattern and sewed with homemade sinew thread. Those designed for ordinary wear around the village usually reach from four to six inches above

An Indian girl making her first pair of moccasins

the ankle; trail boots may be knee high. If they are for "dress up" or a gift, great care is taken to select evenly colored skins, and the tops may be of white caribou, or even of imported calfskin. They are often decorated with beads, and the tops of the boots may be finished with decorative inserts beneath border strips of beaver fur.

Perhaps no fur garment requires more skilled workmanship than a pair of well-made moccasins. At an early age girls are taught all the necessary processes from the tanning of the hide to the final decorative touches. It is a proud day indeed when the Indian girl finishes her first pair of really well-made moccasins and is commended by the expert older women for her tight, sturdy seams,

An elderly Indian making snowshoes

firm welting, beautifully beaded vamps, and even for the colorful crocheted drawstrings—finished off with fluffy pompons—at the tops of the boots.

Like the Eskimos, Indian men and boys are busy too the year round. When fathers are not working for wages they are hunting,

Father and son making a dog sled

fishing, or trapping, helping to build a house, or getting a supply of fuel or ice. There is always a sled or a boat, hunting equipment or household furniture to be made or repaired.

In an Indian family the boys must learn many things from their

A pack dog

father. At home they help to make and repair a boat, sleds, snowshoes, fish traps, and fish wheels. They may help to make a cabin or a cache. Sometimes it is their special job to keep the woodbox and the water barrel filled. On the trail they learn how to pitch a tent and make a warm camp in the deep snow and bitter cold of the Arctic; they help with simple cooking over a campfire. Important lessons also are: how to manage a dog team on the trail, and how to care for the dogs in camp. The boys must also become

A village council meeting

adept at making emergency repairs on broken dog harnesses or sleds. When hunting, they learn to recognize tracks and to follow and shoot different kinds of game. At camp they must become responsible for the proper care of guns and hunting gear. They help to set traps, skin the fur animals, and care for the pelts. Finally, they are taught how to break camp and pack the sled; also how to make and lash a pack onto a pack dog. Always they must be alert, quick to recognize danger; oftentimes being able to make the right decision quickly can save the life of a dog—perhaps the whole team—or even that of a human being!

Village life in the Interior, as in other native villages, is a democratic way of life. A chief and council elected yearly by the people

A social gathering at the schoolhouse

of the village manage the business affairs of the little community. A council may spend hours helping people combine or "pool" their grocery orders, so the village may get lower prices on a big order through the trader or even from an outside source. Organizing a cooperative store is an affair to be handled by the council. Many minor matters are also considered, such as controlling loose dogs, dealing with small thefts in the community, finding homes for orphaned children, and maintaining good working relationships with missionaries, teachers, fur dealers, and others.

The schoolhouse is usually the center where council meetings, community meetings, and social affairs are held. Frequently games and dances are enjoyed at the schoolhouse. Two or three of the

Baby held to mother's back with a beaded "baby strap"

men and boys are likely to have violins and guitars, and a portable phonograph helps to provide music for the dances.

There are many special programs at the school. Christmas, Thanksgiving, Memorial Day, and certain church holidays are observed, either at the school or in the village church building. If game and food have been scarce, the killing of a moose becomes an occasion for quiet celebration. Prayers of thanksgiving are offered and the people enjoy an indoor picnic. Every able-bodied person attends these affairs; even the tiniest baby is wrapped in a

A village church service

blanket and strapped to its mother's back. No baby-sitters are needed, for baby goes too.

The village church building is seldom more than a large cabin provided with wooden benches and a platform or simple altar at the front of the room. The Indian people are very devout and attend their church services regularly whenever they are in the village. The Episcopal, Presbyterian, and Catholic groups are among the religious denominations which have been established in the villages of the Interior for many years. In villages where there is no resident priest or missionary, services are often con-

Galena cemetery

ducted by a "lay minister"—one of the Indian men who has been taught how to conduct a simple service and to represent the church. The people give generously of their meager earnings and labor in supporting these missions. Parts of the Bible and prayer books have been translated into several Indian dialects.

Like most Alaska natives, these calm and serene people believe that "To die is as natural as to be born." When a villager dies, friends and neighbors make the simple coffin and comfort and console the family. If a missionary is in the village he conducts the funeral. Otherwise, the lay reader, teacher, or anyone else who can read well performs a simple burial service. In midwinter the dead cannot be buried in the hard, frozen ground of Interior Alaska, so their bodies in the coffins are placed in a cache until spring. Then they are put into permanent graves. Miniature houses were once built over these graves; in the houses were placed many of the possessions of the deceased in the belief that these would be used by the spirits of the departed in the afterworld. This old custom has practically disappeared. Most graves today are marked by simple wooden crosses.

Besides the church activities and the programs at the schoolhouse there are other occasions which bring the villagers together like a big family—just for amusement. On a quiet winter day everybody may feel like getting out-of-doors for a romp. Sometimes a group made up of people of all ages may have an exciting game of kick-ball. The ball is cleverly fashioned of skin and stuffed with firmly packed moose or caribou hair; sometimes a hair-stuffed moose bladder about the size and weight of a volley ball is used. Fathers, mothers, grandmothers, and baby brothers—the whole family, in fact—find places in a large circle, and everyone does his part to keep the ball kicked back toward the other side of the circle. Sometimes a ball is kept flying, sliding, skidding, and bouncing for several moments before it is lost outside the circle.

Almost everybody loves the sled-dog puppies—small round balls of soft fur. The children spend many hours romping with these playful, frisky animals, and can hardly wait until they can begin to "break them in" to harness. Most native dogs in Interior Alaska are known as Malemutes. These are fairly large dogs, with strong bodies, thick grayish-brown and white fur, and bushy tails. Some say that these dogs originally came from wolf stock. They certainly

Sled-dog puppies

resemble wolves in many respects, and even today some of the sled dogs in the more isolated villages are known to be half wolf; they are savage and must be handled with care. However, an ordinary Malemute pup, treated with kindness and well fed, can be a very desirable household pet.

At the end of each day there is a chorus of yelping as the dog teams return to the village. The tired, hungry dogs are unharnessed and chained to their individual hitching posts before each is tossed its daily ration of dry fish. Indoors, the last chores are finished. The water barrel is full and kindling is made for the morning fire.

The Northern Lights

Damp moccasins and insoles are set near the stove to dry. By the light of a kerosene lamp, or the brighter Coleman lamp, the family finishes its simple evening meal. Guns and hunting equipment are checked and plans are made for tomorrow.

Snug in their sleeping bags, the children can hear the distant howl of a wolf or the soft rustle of the flames in the wood stove. Soon the village sleeps peacefully under the great flowing, wavering curtain of the Northern Lights.

CHAPTER VIII

The Larger Towns

Men rushing to Alaska in 1898 to prospect for gold found that travel was slow and dangerous. It took longer to go from Seattle to Juneau than it now takes to go around the world. Today one can leave Seattle in the morning in a comfortable airliner and be in Nome on the evening of the same day. Throughout the trip the pilot will be "on the beam," for Alaska is now covered with beam stations and other aids to aerial navigation. If one is on his way to Japan, China, or Korea, he may fly directly from Seattle to Anchorage, then westward along the Aleutian chain.

Many of the pioneers and old-timers of Alaska enjoyed their isolation—their "kingdoms in the wilderness." Today they are astonished, and often a bit sad, to hear the roaring of the big airplane motors, and to see quantities of construction materials and military supplies coming into their once secluded homeland.

There are many new faces. The population of Alaska almost tripled between 1940 and 1956. No longer are Anchorage and Fairbanks merely mining and construction camps, or supply centers. Modern conveniences have made these larger Alaskan towns very much like small cities in the States today. The public buildings, churches, shops, apartment houses, sidewalks, paved streets, and

Anchorage

automobiles—all seem familiar and cosmopolitan. At the movies, in a comfortable hotel, in a restaurant, or in a modern home with radio and television, a visitor is likely to feel very much at home in Alaska's metropolitan centers.

However, there are a few differences. Over Alaskan cities the skies are almost constantly vapor-streaked by planes winging their way to and from the two hundred and fifty airfields and forty sea bases of the Territory. Air Force jets on patrol and training flights are commonplace. In an interior town during the winter most people wear parkas and fur boots. An occasional dog team slithers through the streets, the sled runners crunching in the snow and the driver shouting at the dogs—a startling contrast to the modern automobile traffic that shares the street with the dogs.

Anchorage, with 30,000 persons, is the largest city in Alaska. Since there are 30,000 more people in the suburbs, there are actually 60,000 persons in the metropolitan area. In 1914 this town was only a construction camp for the Alaska Railroad. Now it is actually the hub of the Territory—the center of a spider web of airlines that stretch out all over Alaska and connect with transcontinental routes from the United States to the Orient. Near Anchorage are Fort Richardson, Alaska Department Headquarters of the Army, and Elmendorf Field. The main office and car shops of the Alaska Railroad are also located in Anchorage. Many people believe that this city should become the capital of Alaska. Only a few Indians or Eskimos are seen here; Anchorage is almost entirely a white man's town.

Fairbanks is the transportation, business, and medical center of the interior and northern parts of Alaska. The population of this town—including its suburbs—is approximately 35,000 persons. Here is the northern terminal of the Alaska Railroad. From Fairbanks, highways stretch to the southern coast, to the Yukon River, to Canada, and to the States. Airlines connect all the small interior villages with this inland center. Planes leave Fairbanks regularly to make weather observations over the North Pole. Two large air bases are located near the city. Only a hundred miles to the southeast, at Fort Greeley, the Army maintains an Arctic test base and training center. Like Anchorage, Fairbanks has modern hotels and apartment buildings, churches, shops, theaters, and television towers. However, here there are many log cabins mixed with the frame houses, and Indians and Eskimos are seen on the streets. The pungent odor of burning spruce wood, as well as other reminders of frontier days, afford for the visitor a suggestion of pioneer life.

Near Fairbanks is the University of Alaska—the world's farthest-north college. Recently three branches of the university, called community colleges, have been established near Anchorage, Juneau, and Ketchikan. Many fields of specialization are offered;

Fairbanks

however, the School of Mines and the Agricultural Experimental Stations are especially well known. The university also conducts valuable and popular extension programs throughout Alaska.

The excellent University Museum exhibits specimens of prehistoric mastodon and mammoth tusks and bones, as well as bones of the saber-toothed cat, the short-faced bear, and other prehistoric animals that have been collected from the placer mines. Many arrowheads, stone axes, and other artifacts dug from the ruins of ancient Eskimo villages are displayed in this museum too.

Juneau, located in the panhandle of the Territory, is the capital of Alaska. Since it has an excellent harbor, it is also the home port

Juneau

of many fishing boats and motor ships. Most territorial offices are located here, including the governor's office. Here also the territorial legislature—sixteen senators and twenty-four representatives—meets every other year. Many United States government offices have headquarters in Juneau, such as the Forest Service, Fish and Wildlife Service, Bureau of Indian Affairs, and the Department of Labor. The city has a public library and a most interesting Alaska Historical Museum, where visitors may enjoy countless hours in the midst of totemic figures, mounted specimens of Alaskan birds and animals, native baskets, artifacts, and many objects of historical interest. The genial curator adds much to one's apprecia-

Mendenhall Glacier

tion of Alaska history and native customs from his own wide experience in the Territory.

Juneau is beautifully located at the base of steep, towering mountains. A scenic mountain trail winds steeply upward behind the city; from above timberline on Mt. Roberts one may enjoy a sea-gull's view of the narrow Gastineau Channel and of the town itself, far below, crowded onto a narrow ruffle of land little more than half a mile wide.

It is only twelve miles from Juneau to the famous Mendenhall Glacier. Here icy, silt-laden glacial streams rush out from black caverns hidden under the overhanging cliffs of blue ice. In fair

Ketchikan

weather dozens of picnickers use the fireplaces and tables in the nearby recreation areas provided by the United States Forest Service.

Ketchikan, with a population of 7500 persons, is Alaska's southernmost city. Like Juneau, it huddles on a narrow strip of land at the foot of a steep mountain, and it has a good harbor. Because it is the first Alaskan city on the steamer lane from Seattle it is often called the "First City." However, Ketchikan has an even more distinctive name—"the Salmon Capital of the World." It has a dozen or more canneries that pack about twenty-four million cans of salmon a year!

But fishing is not the only important industry of this remarkable small city. A tremendous pulp mill—one of the largest in the world —has recently been completed here, at a cost of fifty-two million dollars. It covers fifty-three acres of land. The huge mill produces about four hundred tons of pulp daily. Bales of the dried pulp are shipped by ocean freight to ports all over the world, to be made into fine quality rayon, cellophane, nitrocellulose, and paper.

Tourists visiting Ketchikan are greatly impressed by the totem poles in the City Park, and by those in the Totem Park at Saxman, two miles farther south along the scenic shoreline. Many of these poles were reconstructed by Indian craftsmen several years ago as a public-works project, to help relieve unemployment.

It is only a short cruise by motor launch or fishing boat to nearby Annette Island, where a group of prosperous Tsimpseans live in modern homes in the village of Metlakatla. Shortly before 1900 a group of Canadian Indians, under the leadership of the famous missionary Father Duncan, obtained permission from the United States government to establish this village. Now the Metlakatlans own a cooperative cannery and store.

Sitka is another small, modern town on Baranof Island, in southeastern Alaska. It is in a beautiful setting, with many tiny islands dotting the surrounding sea, and snow-capped Mt. Edgecumbe rising in the background. Founded by the Russians in 1799, Sitka became the trading center and the most important city in all Alaska. For sixty years there was great hostility between the Indians and the Russians, who nevertheless maintained firm control. The village flourished as the capital of Russian America until the Territory was purchased by the United States in 1867. Here the formal transfer took place; the Imperial flag of Russia was hauled down and the Stars and Stripes raised in its place.

Even now, there are many reminders of the Russian occupation in Sitka, such as the old Russian Orthodox Greek Catholic Cathedral. Occasionally a visitor is permitted to climb the narrow staircase to the belfry to see the ancient Russian bronze bells and to

Sitka and nearby Mt. Edgecumbe School and Medical Center on Japonski Island form a single community. Mt. Edgecumbe is in the background

enjoy the view of the town, the mountains, and the lagoon. An ancient Russian-built orphange at Sitka still serves as a residence for the Bishop of the church. In various places about town, as well as in other parts of Alaska, there are old cannons called "pushka." These are grim reminders not only of the early battles but also of the fact that Alaska might even now be behind the Iron Curtain if the United States had not bought the Territory from Russia soon after the Civil War.

The Sitka National Park contains some of the finest totem poles in the Territory, as well as an old Russian fort and blockhouse. The Home for Alaska Pioneers, maintained for dependent old persons, is in Sitka. Here also is the Sheldon Jackson School—named for a renowned missionary—with a full high-school program. Across the channel from Sitka are the Mt. Edgecumbe Vocational

A "pushka"

School, a tuberculosis sanitarium, and Alaska's only orthopedic hospital, all of them Federal institutions.

The larger towns in all parts of Alaska suffer from a housing shortage. In the rapidly growing towns it is almost impossible to rent or buy a house at any price. Hotel and boarding-house rates are extremely high. Consequently, hundreds of makeshift shelters have been built; these shack-towns constitute slums that are the equal of slums anywhere for filth, fire and health hazards, and community disgrace. But in spite of high costs, there are many middle-class homes and a few luxury homes in every Alaskan city.

Food, too, is expensive in the Territory, since most of the basic commodities must be imported from the States. Some of the modern markets offer a tempting variety of foods brought in by air. In southeastern Alaskan cities the shopper can buy fish, crab, and shrimps from the markets or direct from the fishermen. Hunters may bring in an occasional treat of venison, moose meat, or wild ducks to their friends, but a wise law prohibits the sale of game in the stores. Gardening is a popular activity, both as a hobby and as a practical, economical way of securing a few vegetables—potatoes, carrots, turnips, cabbage, and greens—for the family larder.

Police and fire protection, hospitals, public-welfare programs, public schools, radio and television, newspapers—all the community facilities and conveniences found in small cities in the States are established in the larger Alaskan towns. Electricity, telephone, water, fuel oil and coal, garbage disposal, and taxi service are available, but such utilities and services are more expensive in Alaska than they are in the States, partly because of greater shipping costs and labor charges.

Larger-town recreational facilities are many. Cocktail bars, "juke joints," and dine-and-dance establishments are gay throughout the year, crowded with Sourdoughs, Cheechakos, and happy visitors. Dinner jackets and party dresses are "musts" for formal receptions and dances, especially in the capital city. Home dinner parties and card parties are common. Radio and television also provide entertainment in many homes. National and international societies, lodges, and clubs—both men's and women's organizations—have established chapters and units in the larger towns of Alaska. The Boy Scouts, the Girl Scouts, and the 4-H Clubs are very active. Photography fans organize clubs; so do amateur writers and artists. There are bridge clubs, sewing clubs, square-dance clubs, ski clubs, yacht clubs, and a long list of other special-interest groups.

In the interior towns skating, skiing, and dog-racing are among the most popular sports. Dog races are held each winter in Nome, Fairbanks, and Anchorage, where the cold, dry weather and snow provide excellent conditions. Drivers bring in their teams from miles around. A contestant in an outlying village may arrange for a bush pilot to come for him and his team—everything is loaded into the plane: sled, dogs, dog food, and driver! Some drivers bring

A dog-racing team

in their dogs and sleds by truck; those from nearby villages may drive their teams into the city. The prizes are big, and excitement runs high. Camera-happy crowds line the barricades at the finish line to cheer the winner and take dozens of pictures. Photography shops are packed with "shutterbugs" and sports fans, all chatting excitedly about the big events while waiting for their snapshots of favorite teams and drivers.

The Nenana Ice Pool is probably one of the world's greatest jackpots—a person can win thousands of dollars if he guesses right! From December on through the winter everybody talks about it, from one end of the Territory to the other. Sourdoughs,

Nenana Ice Pool

Cheechakos, Eskimos, Indians—everyone pays his dollar per ticket, and writes in his guess as to the date, hour, and minute when the "break-up" will occur. Then the tickets are sent to the Ice Pool headquarters. Each ticket-owner keeps the numbered stubs of his tickets, to claim the jackpot he feels sure he will win. The old-timers watch the depth of the ice, the average winter temperature, the habits of wildlife—things that point to a long cold winter or an early spring. They hope these signs will help them to guess the date of the break-up.

The ice breaks up at many different dates and hours at different places in the Territory. So, for the purposes of the Ice Pool, there must be one official break-up time. This is recorded on a special clock at the little village of Nenana. Well before break-up time a strong post is braced upright in the ice of the Nenana River; this spot is just a few yards upstream from a wire stretched across the river. The official break-up time is recorded when the ice moves downstream and the post touches the wire; this stops the clock which is safely housed on the nearby bank.

From the time the post starts moving until it stops the clock all Alaska listens in suspense to radio broadcasts which describe in great detail the progress of this instrument of Lady Luck. It is as exciting as the last inning of the deciding game of the World Series. If the ice jams and sticks before the post hits the wire, the suspense may last for several hours or even days! When the clock finally stops, and the owner of the lucky ticket is known, thousands of disappointed losers tear up their ticket stubs—"Better luck next year!"

Basketball is a favorite sport. Many Alaskan tournaments are arranged in certain areas. The teams travel by plane or boat. Curling and hockey teams in Fairbanks play international matches with contesting teams from Canada. Baseball is common, particularly softball. Baseball fans who can afford to do so often plan a trip to the States each fall to see the World Series.

Salmon-fishing is probably the most popular sport in southeastern Alaska. A boy in a small skiff fishing close to shore may catch a king salmon that weighs half as much as he does. Girls, too, are often good fishermen and become very skillful at coaxing

Landing a catch

the salmon to take their bait. Fishing trips are often a family affair. Occasionally several families charter a small boat and go out for an entire day. The skipper of the boat is also the guide. He knows where the good fishing spots are to be found. From May to

September many fishing parties are out each weekend, rain or shine, trying for "kings" or "cohoes" with light tackle.

In the cities of southeastern Alaska the great sports events of the season are the Salmon Derbies. For the winners, prizes ranging from beautiful aluminum boats with outboard motors, down to sport clothes and picnic kits, are on display in shop windows long before Derby Day. Contestants register on official blanks and pay their entrance fees.

Finally the day dawns—it is probably raining, as is usual in this part of Alaska, but who cares? Fishermen get into slickers and boots, pick up their sandwiches and fishing-tackle boxes, and hurry to the dock to join their parties. Some will stop by at the cold-storage plant and pick up the necessary blocks of frozen herring for bait. When everything is safely stowed aboard, the boats shove off in an atmosphere warm with excitement, in spite of the morning chill. Soon the galley stoves are going; then come the doughnuts and mugs of hot coffee—never more welcome! But as the boats chug on nearer to the fishing grounds, the joking fishermen break away from the warmth of the cabins; they brave the chilly deck breezes to start cutting bait, and—most important—to arrange the sinkers, spoons, hooks, and finally the bait on their lines exactly right.

Every fisherman has his bait in the water the moment the contest is officially open. Derby officials on fast boats cruise through the fishing grounds to make sure that all contestants observe the rules, as well as to weigh the fish and establish the order of the prizes. Too soon the exciting day is over and hundreds of fishermen gather to hear the last official announcements. There are cheers and backslapping for the winners; consolation and teasing for the unfortunate ones who caught only tomcod and bullheads; skeptical smiles for those who lost "the biggest one of all!"

But win or lose, Derby or no Derby, there is positively no thrill like the excitement that possesses an angler, man or woman, when a forty-pound king lunges away with the bait, or a lightning-fast

A Salmon Derby catch

cohoe strikes the hook and jumps clear of the water in a mad struggle to snap himself free. Then the fisherman springs into action. Every muscle responds as he braces his feet, clutches his rod, and reels for dear life. No sound is sweeter than the whine of the reel and the whir of the line, and truly no challenge is greater to the skill of a fisherman. "Keep the line tight—don't jerk—give him time!" shout his companions as they hastily reel in their own lines to avoid the possibility of hopeless snarls and tangles. How the lucky angler's heart pounds as he finally pulls his silver giant alongside the boat and skillfully guides it into the hand net, amidst the cheers of his admiring friends! Then the fish is weighed and the suspense is over. Small wonder that fishermen love Alaska!

True, there are a few things that people do for fun in the States that are missing in Alaska. There are many new experiences for Alaska boys and girls when they go "Outside"—to the States—for the first time. They often see their first circus, or ballet, or opera. Perhaps they visit an amusement park, with its merry-go-round, Ferris wheel, and roller coaster. They may visit the zoo for the first time, where they will be pleased to see an old friend, the polar bear. Indeed, these are all exciting things to do, and they add much to the thrill of a vacation trip. But few people who have lived long in Alaska are content to make their home elsewhere, even in the States, where there are so many attractions and such a variety of things to do. It is wonderful to visit the States and other lands, but the biggest thrill of all is to get back home again to Alaska—the land of fish, fur, and frost; of forests, sea, and mountains; of snug villages and lonely tundra; of sturdy, resourceful people living in harmony with the conditions nature provides.